THE ORIGIN OF RELIGION

The
Origin of Religion:
Evolution or Revelation

BASED ON THE SMYTH LECTURES
DELIVERED AT COLUMBIA THEOLOGICAL SEMINARY
DECATUR, GEORGIA, 1935

Third and Revised Edition.

BY SAMUEL MARINUS ZWEMER, D.D., Litt. D.,

PROFESSOR EMERITUS OF THE HISTORY OF
RELIGION AND CHRISTIAN MISSIONS
AT PRINCETON THEOLOGICAL
SEMINARY

WIPF & STOCK · Eugene, Oregon

Wipf and Stock Publishers
199 W 8th Ave, Suite 3
Eugene, OR 97401

The Origin of Religion
Evolution or Revelation
By Zwemer, Samuel M.
ISBN 13: 978-1-62032-034-1
Publication date 3/1/2012
Previously published by Loizeaux, 1945

DEDICATED BY PERMISSION
TO
P. WILHELM SCHMIDT, S.V.D.

Professor at the University of Vienna
Distinguished Scholar and Anthropologist
Founder and Editor of "Anthropos"
Author of many books on
the Origin and Growth of Religion
and whose great work on "The Origin of the Idea of God"
will ever remain a monument of
erudition and suggestive thought

CONTENTS

INTRODUCTION 11
The literature on this subject is abundant, but much of it is anti-theistic. The vastness of the stellar universe and its age do not reduce the importance of man as observer. Argument of the book in outline. Based not primarily on Scripture but on anthropology by the historical method. The history of religion from this viewpoint.

I. THE HISTORY OF ORIGINS IN RELIGION . . . 19
The problem of the origin of man closely related. His antiquity. The unity of the race. Religion as old as humanity. Theistic and anti-theistic theories in conflict. History of religion defined. Its precursors and protagonists. Max Müller and later. Present status. The Bible as sourcebook. The great living religions and Christianity. Its finality.

II. THE ORIGIN OF RELIGION 51
Evolution or revelation. Earlier theories no longer adequate. Andrew Lang's theory. Wilhelm Schmidt. His method. The primitive High-gods. Boegner. Du Bois. Renouf. Marett. The religion of the Stone Age. Le Roy. Five elements in all primitive religion: the family, the High-god, conscience, belief in immortality, prayer, and sacrifice.

III. THE ORIGIN OF THE IDEA OF GOD 75
Andrew Lang's Sky-gods. Schmidt's work on the subject. Further evidence from every area of primitive culture. The character of the High-gods. Among American Indians. In Africa. China. The Isokos. Sumatra. Monotheism in ethnic religions. China. Japan. Egypt. Assyria. Arabia. India. How explain this. The subjective and objective factors in origin of idea of God. Francis L. Patton and John Calvin quoted.

IV. THE ORIGIN OF THE WORLD AND OF MAN . . 101
Myths regarding creation widespread and significant. Four possible theories. Evolution and Emanation not as common

as Creation among primitives. Maori poem. Tahiti hymn. Creation myths collated by Schmidt. Among American Indians. Andaman Islanders. The Pygmies. The Ainus. Semangs. Samoyeds. Cosmogony of ethnic religions. Assyria and Babylonia. Persia. India. Similarity to account in Genesis. The origin of man in these myths due to special creation. Origin of evil in the world. Golden Age is in the past. Walter Lippman quoted. The Bible as key to the creation-myths of the race.

V. THE ORIGIN OF PRAYER AND SACRIFICE . . 125

Prayer the oldest and most universal religious rite. Its motive and character. Among ancient Greeks and Romans. Heiler on the prayer of primitives. Prayer was prior to magic. Posture and its significance. Examples of prayer. Delaware Indian. Khonds. In Africa. Algonquin Indians. Arapahos. Chinese Emperor. Origin of Sacrifice. E. O. James' opinion. The idea of substitution. Classification of sacrifices. Examples. Is it due to totemism? The Semites not totemistic. The reference to its origin in Genesis.

VI. THE ORIGIN OF FIRE-WORSHIP AND FIRE AS A SYMBOL OF DEITY 151

Early association of fire with worship. Crawley's statement. (1) Fire in the Bible narrative as symbol of Deity. In Jewish tradition. In primitive religion. Its various forms. Origin of fire in human culture. Legends regarding its origin. Prometheus. Agni. The story as told by the Indians. Maoris. Bantus. (2) Fire-gods in Mexico. In Japan. Sun-worship. Zoroastrian worship of fire. Agni and the hearth. China. The Yezdis. The Vestal virgins. (3) Fire as method of communion by flame, smoke, or incense. The hearth as sacred. Antiquity of incense-trade. (4) Fire-baptism and ordeal. The halo as symbol of divine favor. Moses' face. The halo in art. Our God is a consuming fire.

VII. THE ORIGIN OF MARRIAGE AND PRIMITIVE ETHICS 179

The so-called cave-man's religion. Newberry and Lewis Browne. Antiquity of family-life. Theory of promiscuity and tribal marriage supported and also opposed by anthropologists. Malinowsky and Westermarck on monogamy as earliest form of marriage and in every area of primitive culture. Incest a crime. Crowley on primitive marriage. Grosse. Seligmann. The origin of the moral idea. The dawn of conscience. Faith, hope, and charity in primitive

CONTENTS

religion. Loyalty and mother-love. Not emergent evolution but innate. The moral law. Examples. The Supreme Being author of moral code. *Homo sapiens*.

VIII. THE ORIGIN OF BELIEF IN IMMORTALITY . 207
This belief one of strongest moral sanctions. Universal and ancient. Love is stronger than death. Etruscan tombs. The Jains. Sir James Frazer. This belief in Israel. Among primitives. Burial rites. Mourning customs. Antiquity of this belief. Calling the dead. Origin of this faith in immortality. Palimpsest of primitive revelation. Future life in a better world. Primitive eschatology includes reward and punishment hereafter. The gospel of the Resurrection. The otherworldly character of all religions. Of Christianity. Alexander Whyte quoted.

L'ENVOI BY PROFESSOR SCHMIDT 233

CLASSIFIED SELECT BIBLIOGRAPHY 239

INDEX 249

INTRODUCTION

THERE IS NO DEARTH OF LITERATURE ON THE ORIGIN and growth of religion, as is evident from the vast bibliography of the subject. Most of the popular works, however, especially those of the nineteenth century, are based on an evolutionary hypothesis regarding the origin of man, and in many cases they took for fact another hypothesis which eliminated God from human history. This book is written in the firm faith that God is the creator of the universe and that he made man in his image.

The universe is undoubtedly very large and very old. The whole sidereal system is a mere unit of measurement in the curvature of space, although it is said to contain between thirty thousand and a hundred thousand million stars. Light could pass from one end to the other only in 100,000 years! And this is only one among a million or more of similar systems. Yet, as far as science can interpret the facts, our little earth is the only planet in the vast universe where we find rational life.[1] And even as science has made us aware of the almost incredible vastness of the universe in time and space, it has also made us realize its unity. "The

[1] Eddington, *Nature of the Physical World*, p. 170. Jeans, *The Mysterious Universe*, p. 2.

only God in whom a modern western man can believe is one Gold Almighty, maker of heaven and earth"[2] According to Douglass Jerrold, "modern man with his crafts, arts, and social organziation appears suddenly not much earlier than 20,000 B.C., and very possibly as late as 15,000 B.C., and (what was never realized until recently) within a few thousand years of the first appearance of a culture, man is found living in a highly complex society." The problem for scientific inquiry is not the *length* of precultural history, but the facts. Archaeology in giving man a much longer pedigree gave him also a newer pedigree rather than that formerly attributed to the cave-man. The new movement in anthropology is based on the historical method adopted by the late Dr. Rivers at Cambridge, by Professor Graebner and Peter Schmidt in Germany and Austria, by Le Roy in France, and by R. H. Lowie and other American anthropologists. It may yet be proved, as one of these writers states, that "there is, in fact, more sound anthropology in the Old Testament than in all the works of 'modern historians' put together." The fact is that the supposed length of the precultural stage of man's history does not affect the validity of historical inquiry any more than the size of the universe reduces the importance of man—the observer of it.

The *homo sapiens* of the scientist, in any case, appears on the scene already possessed of a religious instinct and exercising religious rites. He is conscious of an unseen world and realizes that death does not end

[2] Sydney Dark, *Orthodoxy Sees It Through*, p. 144.

all. What was the origin and character of his religion? The argument of the lectures that follow can be summarized in a few sentences:

(I) The history of the history of religion reveals two theories, the one theistic, the other anti-theistic, and these are in conflict. It is important, therefore, for all who believe in God and his revelation not to omit the Bible as source-book in the study of origins.

(II) The origin of the idea of God is not by any process of evolution, but by instinct or by an objective-subjective revelation.

(III) The evidence for primitive monotheism is found, not only in every area of primitive culture, but also in the earlier forms of the great ethnic religions.

(IV) The widespread Creation-myths regarding the origin of the world and of man, the so-called Golden Age and the entrance of death, all point to a common tradition regarding man's Creation and the Fall, strangely parallel to the Scriptures.

(V) Prayer and sacrifice are religious rites of such antiquity and universality that their signficance and persistence point to a common origin, namely, in man's desire to restore a lost communion and propitiate God.

(VI) The origin of fire is mysterious and it is everywhere associated with religion and sacrifice. In primitive religion and in ethnic faiths it is a symbol of deity, an object of worship, or a method of communion. The universality of this symbolism and its antiquity point to a common primitive tradition.

(VII) Taboos and totemism, together with the laws

against incest, witness to the early sanctity of marriage and its monogamous character over against the evolutionary theory of early promiscuity. There are evidences of faith, hope, and charity in primitive religion, which can only be explained on the basis of a primitive revelation.

(VIII) Finally, belief in the immortality of the soul is universal among primitives and in nearly all of the Ethnic religions; this other worldly character of man's religious outlook is also proof of primitive revelation.

The argument as outlined above is based, however, not primarily on the Scriptures nor on any dogmatic preconceptions, but on the historical method of investigation. For even as the science of archaeology has proved in so many cases a vindication of the accuracy and historicity of the Pentateuch, so the use of the historic method in anthropology has compelled many to restate their findings on the origin of religion, and the result is more in accord with Scriptures. The evolutionary view has been tied down to the supposed axiom that the higher must always have come later than the lower. The Evolutionist could never see monotheism in the early history of religion; it must always be preceded by polytheism and that, in turn, by animism. Andrew Lang sprang a breach in this rigid wall by revealing the idea of High-gods among primitives. Professor Wilhelm Schmidt in his *Origin of the Idea of God* concludes: "A belief in a Supreme Being is to be found among *all* the peoples of the primitive culture, not indeed everywhere in the same form or the same vigor, but still everywhere prominent enough to make his dominant position indubitable."

Dr. Langdon, Professor of Assyriology at Oxford, makes an equally startling statement in his book, *Semitic Mythology:*

"I may fail to carry conviction in concluding that, both in Sumerian and Semitic religions, monotheism preceded polytheism and belief in good and evil spirits. The evidence and reasons for this conclusion, so contrary to accepted and current views, have been set down with care and with the perception of adverse criticism. It is, I trust, the conclusion of knowledge and not of audacious preconception." (p. xviii.)

And a little later he says:

"Although the South Arabians and Accadians are far advanced beyond the primitive Bedouin stage in the periods when the inscriptions begin, their history shows that it is characteristic of the Semites to use animal names in times of advanced culture, when there is no possible influence of primitive totemism. *I therefore reject the totemistic theory absolutely.* Early Canaanitish and Hebrew religions are far beyond primitive totemism (if it ever existed among them) in the period when any definite information can be obtained about them. . . . . All Semitic tribes appear to have started with a single tribal deity whom they regarded as the Divine Creator of his people." (p. 93.)

Now if this be the case both among primitives in every part of the world and in some of the oldest cultures, Sumerian, Semitic, and Accadian, we can only conclude that the history of religion has been one of decline and degeneration, rather than of evolution and unbroken ascent.

Dr. Schmidt sums up his conclusions in two paragraphs which at the outset of our discussion may well challenge attention, if they do not produce conviction. His words are a striking parallel to Paul's statement in the first chapter of his epistle to the Romans:

"As external civilization increased in splendour and wealth, so religion came to be expressed in forms of ever-increasing magnificance and opulence. Images of gods and daimones multiplied to an extent which defies all classification. Wealthy temples, shrines, and groves arose; more priests and servants, more sacrifices and ceremonies were instituted. But all this cannot blind us to the fact that despite the glory and wealth of the outward forms, the inner kernel of religion often disappeared and its essential strength was weakened. The results of this, both moral and social, were anything but desirable, leading to extreme degradation and even to the deification of the immoral and antisocial. The principal cause of this corruption was that the figure of the Supreme Being was sinking further and further into the background, hidden behind the impenetrable phalanx of the thousand new gods and daimones. . . . .

"But all the while, the ancient primitive religion still continued among the few remainders of the primitive culture, preserved by fragmentary peoples driven into the most distant regions. Yet in their condition of stagnation, poverty, and insignificance, even there it must necessarily have lost much of its power and greatness, so that even among such peoples it is much too late to find a true image of the faith of really primitive men. It remains for us, by

INTRODUCTION

dint of laborious research, to put gradually together from many faded fragments a lifelike picture of this religion."[3]

We have attempted to collate the results of this laborious research on the part of Dr. Schmidt and other ethnologists, in the chapters that follow, six of which were first given as lectures on the Smyth Foundation at Columbia Theological Seminary, Decatur, Georgia, in March, 1935. It was a privilege and an honor to make some small contribution to this series of lectures, made possible through the generosity of the late Rev. Thomas Smyth, D.D., pastor of the Second Presbyterian Church of Charleston, South Carolina. For the past twenty-three years distinguished scholars have treated a large variety of themes, doctrinal, critical, practical, and archaeological. This was, I believe, the first course on the History of Religion and Its Origin. The classified Bibliography at the end of the volume and the footnotes indicate our sources and will afford an index to the more recent literature for further study.

SAMUEL M. ZWEMER

Princeton, New Jersey

[3] Schmidt, *Origin and Growth of Religion*, pp. 289, 290.

NOTE ON THIRD AND REVISED EDITION

Owing to War conditions and Government Conservation Order No. M99, the plates of this book were melted down in 1942. When the demand for it continued, especially for study-classes in anthropology, this third and revised edition was prepared with full consent of the original publishers. We pray that its message may reach a still wider circle of readers.

S. M. Z.

Nov. 1945.

CHAPTER ONE

THE HISTORY OF ORIGINS IN RELIGION

WHEN we recognize the enormous period of time during which man is now asserted to have evolved on the earth, and compare it with the fact that we have such scanty knowledge of his thoughts as revealed by writing and inferred from cult implements and edifices for any period earlier than 3000 B.C., it is obvious that dogmatism on the subject is wholly impossible. But it is difficult not to feel that it is an impossible task to explain the evolution of religion from magic in any form, and that we must accept as ultimate the religious sentiment. We are, it is true, only gradually emerging from the doctrines of a crude evolutionism, but already it is less fashionable than it was to assert that consciousness is a late epiphenomenon on matter, and we may anticipate that it will eventually be generally accepted that it is unwise to claim that religion is derived from magic and is the creation of minds which had realized that magic could not produce the effects which it was at first believed to be potent to accomplish."

> A. BERRIEDALE KEITH, D.C.L., D.Litt.,
> *Professor of Sanskrit and Comparative Philology at the University of Edinburgh,* in FOREWORD TO THE ORIGIN AND DEVELOPMENT OF RELIGION IN VEDIC LITERATURE, *by P. S. Deshmukh.*

CHAPTER ONE

THE HISTORY OF ORIGINS IN RELIGION

IN DEALING WITH THE QUESTION OF THE GENESIS and growth of religion we necessarily meet the problem of the origin of man and of the world in which he lives. According to a recent writer in a popular magazine, it all began "ten million years ago in the accidental approach of a wandering star which set up such a tidal wave upon our sun as to turn it into a cigar-shaped object which broke up into separate pieces, and our earth was formed out of one of these pieces."[1] But although materialistic philosophy has taught that the origin of the world was an accident, the best scientists now repudiate such theory. "I had rather believe," said Lord Bacon, "all the fables in the Legend and the Talmud and the Koran than that this universal frame is without a mind." We too would rather believe the first verse of Genesis in its majesty and reticence before the mystery of the Universe, "In the beginning God created the heavens and the earth," than accept the dis-

[1] John Langdon-Davis in *Pearson's Magazine,* June, 1934, "Was There a Creation?"

cordant findings of unbelieving mathematicians and geologists. There can be no creation without a Creator and no religion without a god.

Professor Driesch, a leading embryologist of Great Britain, writes a chapter on "The Breakdown of Materialism" in a recent work on design in nature and says, "The machine theory of development or morphogenesis has been completely refuted and the mechanistic theory does not hold in the field of embryology." In the same volume Sir Oliver Lodge has an eloquent passage, noble in its acknowledgment of the Creator:

"In dealing with the universe as a whole we have no prehistoric qualms to contend with, no hesitation about attributing Intelligence to the operations of a distant Mind or Logos. 'In the beginning was the Word.' The mind responsible is still active today, and we have no reason to suppose that it has changed in the least. The material universe has evolved, and has rendered possible a fresh influx of spiritual reality as it attained greater complexity, but the Creator may be the same yesterday, today, and for ever. His design and purpose in bringing the Universe into existence may not be apparent to us; or we may form some hazy conception of it. That is a relative and subjective matter, not of much consequence except to ourselves. But surely we may have faith that there is a Design and Purpose running through it all, and that the ultimate outcome of the present cosmos, and all its manifold puzzles, will be something grander, more magnificent, and more satisfying than anything we unaided can hope to conceive.

"Survey the whole sweep of evolution; the wonder of regulation amid the immensities of the universe beyond the reach of the most powerful telescope; the equal wonder of regulation amid the minutiae of atomic structure and behaviour, far beyond the penetration of the microscope; the emergence of life on the Earth, on the speck of the universe of which we know most; the gradual development of intelligence, of reason, of appreciation of beauty and of power to create beauty, even the transcendent beauty of personal character. A star is no greater than a violet; gravitation as a force cannot transcend love, for love seems incomparably more effective, more forceful than any physical force, lying as it does at the very root of the universe. But it is all one, beginning in the dust and reaching up into persons who can appreciate and create beauty, and feel love—a constantly changing whole, alive, personal. And it doth not yet appear what there shall be." [2]

No longer can Herbert Spencer's Unknowable First Cause be regarded as a sufficient explanation of the work of Creation. "Every house," as Paul says, "is builded by someone, but he that built all things is God." So we begin our investigations by a great affirmation: "Thou Lord in the beginning hast laid the foundations of the earth, and the heavens are the work of thy hands." And we agree with Archbishop Trench that in the study of religion

"The third chapter of Genesis is undoubtedly the most important chapter in the whole Bible. It is the only chapter which, if we could conceive it as being withdrawn, would leave all the rest of Scripture unintelligible. Take away this chapter and you take away the key of knowledge to all the rest of the Bible." [3]

[2] *The Great Design*, ed. Frances Mason. London, 1934.
[3] Sermon preached in Westminster Abbey on Gen. 3: 21.

Modern anthropology deals with the antiquity of man, the problems of race distribution, of language, culture, and religion, and in each of these fields theistic and antitheistic theories are in conflict. Yet on two great conceptions modern scientists are agreed: namely, on the unity of the race and on the essential religious nature of man. Even so the New Testament Scripture points out both of these facts: "God hath made of one all the nations that dwell on earth and all men are seeking after him if haply they may find him" (Acts 17: 26, 27).

The essential unity and solidarity of the human family is proved by anatomy and physiology—it is a physical unity in which there is no essential difference. Ethnology, sociology, and psychology agree that the various races are intellectually and emotionally of the same kind, while the spiritual unity of the race in their varieties of religious experience and in their response to the Gospel is evident from the history of missions.

The fact of this essential unity has been forcibly expressed in a paper on "The Antiquity and Unity of Man" by the late Dr. Warfield:

"The psychological unity of the race is still more manifest. All men of all varieties are psychologically one and prove themselves possessors of the same mental nature and furniture. Under the same influences they function mentally and spiritually in the same fashion, and prove capable of the same mental reactions. They, they all, and they alone, in the whole realm of animal existences manifest themselves as rational and moral natures; so that Mr. Fiske was fully justified when he declared that though

HISTORY OF ORIGINS IN RELIGION

for zoölogical man the erection of a distinct family from the chimpanzee and orang might suffice, 'on the other hand, for psychological man you must erect a distinct kingdom; nay, you must even dichotomize the universe, putting Man on one side and all things else on the other.'

"So far is it from being of no concern to theology, therefore, that it would be truer to say that the whole doctrinal structure of the Bible account of redemption is founded on its assumption that the race of man is one organic whole, and may be dealt with as such. It is because all are one in Adam that in the matter of sin there is no difference, but all have fallen short of the glory of God (Rom. 3:22 ff.), and, as well, that in the new man there cannot be Greek and Jew, circumcision and uncircumcision, barbarian, Scythian, bondman, freeman; but Christ is all and in all (Col. 3:11). The unity of the old man in Adam is the postulate of the unity of the new man in Christ." [4]

It is of great interest, therefore, to note that all of the older classifications and divisions of the human race have been largely discarded. R. R. Marett of Oxford in his textbook on *Anthropology* exclaims:

"Oh for an external race-mark about which there could be no mistake! That has always been a dream of the anthropologist; but it is a dream that shows no signs of coming true. All sorts of tests of this kind have been suggested. Cranium, cranial sutures, frontal process, nasal bones, eye, chin, jaws, wisdom teeth, hair, humerus, pelvis, the heart-line across the hand, calf, tibia, heel, colour, and even smell—all of these external signs, as well as many more, have been thought, separately or together, to afford the crucial test of a man's pedigree." [5]

---
[4] Benjamin Breckenridge Warfield, *Studies in Theology*, pp. 255-258.
[5] R. R. Marett, *Anthropology* (Home University Library), p. 72.

But he goes on to show that there is no real race distinction. "Man is very much alike everywhere from China to Peru. . . . . Race or breed remains something which we cannot at present isolate." [6]

Again, man always has been and is incurably religious. This is the verdict of archaelogy and anthropology. The rude art on the walls of the caves in which the folk of the Stone Age took shelter has religious significance. The graves of the dead testify to their faith in a hereafter. Religion is as old as the oldest records and is universal among the most primitive tribes today.[7]

Anthropological theories of the origin of religion all seem to go wrong mainly because they seek to simplify overmuch. Religion has just as many aspects as human life and the mind of man. Because humanity itself finds its roots in God, religion does also—unless we begin with an anti-theistic bias.[8]

What has been the history of the science of religions? What various theories have been advanced to account for this universal phenomenon that man is incurably religious? To begin with, the History of Religion is incomparatively a new science. So young, in

[6] *Op. cit.*, pp. 91, 92.

[7] C. C. Clemens, *Urgeschichtliche Religion: die Religion der Stein-, Bronze- und Eisenzeit.*. Bonn, 1932. Cf. vol. II for the illustrations. Gaius Glenn Atkins, *Procession of the Gods*, pp. 5-19.

[8] "We nowhere find either a great race or even a division, however unimportant, professing atheism. Two beliefs are practically universal: a belief in beings superior to man and a conviction that the existence of man is not limited to the present life, but that there remains for him a future beyond the grave." Quatrefages, *The Human Species*, third edition, pp. 483, 484.

fact, that, like all infants, it has yet to rise out of its cradle, get rid of its swaddling-clothes, become independent of its mother, and stand on its own feet.

Whereas the science of Christian missions is as old as the book of Acts, for scarcely two generations have scholars spoken of a Science of Religion as distinct from Apologetics, and truly independent and conscious of its aim.

Its cradle was philosophy, which took care of it for over one hundred years. At present, we recall without much enthusiasm those first attempts at a Science of Religion in the rationalistic period of Voltaire and in the later period of Schelling and Hegel. Bunsen and Max Müller were enthusiastic pupils of Schelling, and through them Romantic philosophy gave impulse to studies that were a decisive factor in the study of the History of Religion.[9] Because the science was so new and arose at a time when Rationalism was the vogue in philosophy, Christian theologians as well as the Christian public were at first unwilling to give it a place. Many felt with Principal Fairbairn (although he spoke of anthropology) that "there is no field where competent instructors are so few and so rare, where unlearned authorities are so many and so rash, and whose testimonies are so contradictory, or so apt to dissolve under analysis into airy nothings."[10]

Archbishop Söderblom and others have sought to draw a distinction between the History of *Religion*

[9] Cf. Edw. Lehmann, "The Evolution of the History of Religion" in the *Revue d'Histoire et de Philosophie Religieuse*, vol. ix, no. 6.
[10] Quoted in the *Princeton Theological Review*, vol. xix, p. 704.

and the History of *Religions*.[11] *The History of Religion*, they say, proposes to show the essential unity of the psychological phenomena called religion and it makes research for the reasons of this unity, which manifests itself under such varied forms in the course of ages among different races and different peoples; and because the History of Religion presupposes a unity in such development, it, generally speaking, accepts the evolutionary hypothesis as the basis of that unity and denies the unique caharacter of the Revelation of God in the Old and New Testament Scriptures, although this also might well form such a basis of unity.

On the other hand, the *History of Religions*, they say, traces the development of each religion to its own sources. These sources are often borrowed one from the other, and the various religions show degeneration and deterioration as well as progressive cultural development. This proposed distinction in the use of the singular and plural noun is, however useful, largely academic. Both terms are used indiscriminately by good authorities. In the literature on the subject, the titles "History of Religion" and "History of Religions" cover the same general ground.

The Science of Religion in its wider sense may conveniently be divided into three main divisions or departments, and these, chronologically stated, are as follows: The History of Religion, The Comparison of Religions, The Philosophy of Religion. The first

[11] *Manuel d'Histoire des Religions,* Paris, 1925, p. 2.

HISTORY OF ORIGINS IN RELIGION   29

collects and classifies the facts; the second compares the data; and the third draws conclusions in the realm of philosophy. The History of Religion in its widest significance, therefore, includes all three. It is "an account of the origin, development, and characteristic features of all religions from those of the lowest savage tribes to those of the most cultivated nations."[12] Is it not therefore almost impossible for a Christian to approach the subject with an empty mind and without any preconceptions? "If the Gospel is a revelation of the Eternal, through facts of time, it cannot be treated simply as one religion among others. Given the revelation of God, Comparative Religion may help to show us how the forms of human nature clothed it with religions of men; but the application of Comparative Religion to the Revelation itself is a fundamental error."[13]

The history of Islam, for example, is not the evolution of a people from animism to monotheism, but of a people, once monotheistic, under the influence of a new religion (which was nevertheless in part old), and which borrowed elements from Christianity and Judaism as well as from Arabian paganism.

What has been the history of the History of Religions? It is a long story, for we agree with Brünner that the heart of the history of humanity is the history of religions.[14] All the ancient civilizations re-

[12] Philip Schaff, *Theological Propadeutic*, p. 19.
[13] Henry M. Gwatkin, *Early Church History*, vol. i, p. 564.
[14] "La Philosophie de la Religion de M. Brünner," by Philippe Bridel, in *Revue de Theologie et de Philosophie*, March, 1930.

30   HISTORY OF ORIGINS IN RELIGION

vealed by archaeology found their root in religious beliefs. If we define religion as "the ensemble of beliefs, obligations, and practices by which man recognizes the supernatural world, performs his duties toward it, and asks help from it," then religion is as old as the oldest records and remains of man.[15]

"No one any longer believes," says Reinach, "that even quaternary man was ignorant of religion; unless we admit the gratuitous and puerile hypothesis of a primitive revelation we must seek the origin of religions in the psychology of man, not of civilized man, but of man the farthest removed."[16]

That is the issue, clearly stated by a representative of the rationalistic and evolutionary school. "The puerile hypothesis" of revelation or the assumption of evolution; God or man; supernaturalism or naturalism. Alas, in the writing of the History of Religions, unbelief and rationalism have had the largest share and, especially during the past century, "This Science seems to have been conducted in a deliberately anti-Christian spirit."[17]

We are indebted to Dr. Lehmann of the University of Lund for an excellent summary of the history of this branch of learning.[18] Centuries before Christ, Herodotus (481 B.C.) and Plutarch, not to speak of Berosos (250 B.C.), gave sketches of the history of

[15] Le Roy, *Religion of the Primitives*, p. 3.
[16] *Cults, Myths, and Religions*, p. 30.
[17] Le Roy, *op. cit.*, p. 8.
[18] "Zur Geschichte der Religions-Geschichte," in 4th edition of Chantepie de la Saussaye's *Lehrbuch der Religions-Geschichte*, vol. 1, pp. 1-22.

HISTORY OF ORIGINS IN RELIGION

various religions and described the customs of foreign nations. Strabo, about the time of Christ, is the first critical writer who deals with the religions of the Orient. He was followed by Varro (died 27 B.C.) and Tacitus.

When we turn to Christian writers, the first important name is that of Augustine. In his book *The City of God* he considers the heathen religions to be the work of the Devil; nevertheless he quotes from non-Christian writers, especially from those who represent Rome and Manicheism. Among medieval writers only the Scandinavian Saxo (1220) and the Icelander Snorri (1241) are remarkable for their contribution on the religions of Northern Europe.

Roger Bacon (1294) wrote a large work on Pagan Religions and Islam. About the time of Bacon, Mangy Khan in Mongolia and the Emperor Akbar (1542-1605) in India held congresses of religion in which Jews, Moslems, Christians, Hindus, Buddhists, etc., took part. These were the precursors of the Parliament of Religions held in Chicago.

It is interesting to note that among the earliest histories of religion are those written by Mohammedans in their books on geography and general history. The outstanding name is that of Mohammed Abdul-Karim Shahrastani of Khorasan, Persia, whose well-known work (A.D. 1153) was translated into German and English, and is the first real History of Religions in world literature. Writing from the Moslem standpoint, he divides all religions as follows: Moslems;

People of the Book (Jews and Christians); those who have a revelation but are not included in class two; and lastly, freethinkers and philosophers.[19] Similar works appeared in India in the fourteenth century, but they are inferior in character.

Marco Polo, who visited Central Asia in 1271 and spent seventeen years in his travels, added much to the knowledge of Oriental Religions in Europe in his day. Meanwhile, Spanish and Portuguese writers also described the religions of Mexico and Peru at the time of their conquests. A Dutch traveler, Bosman, lifted the veil of paganism on the Guinea coast (1798) and the Frenchman, Charles Brosses, wrote the first book on Fetishism in 1760.

At the time of the Reformation and the Renaissance, Erasmus wrote on the heathen origin of certain elements in the Catholic cult and teaching, and John Toland wrote on the same subject (1696) in his book *Christianity Not Mysterious*. Along this path rationalism then began its theory of the origin of religion (in opposition to the statements of Paul in Romans and than of the Church Fathers) by denying an original revelation. David Hume's *Natural History of Religion* (1757) and Voltaire's *Essay* (1780) are typical. German rationalism is represented by Müllers and Creuzer at the beginning of the nineteenth century. They were followed by Schelling and Hegel.

The second period (before we speak of the real

[19] Translated by W. Cureton (2 vol., London, 1846) under the title *Book of Religions and Philosophical Sects* (Al Millal wa'l nahal). German translation of Haarbrücker (Halle, 1850).

founder of the modern science, Max Müller, 1823-1900) is marked by a new phase of historical investigation on the part of Orientalists who specialized in one or more aspects of the subject, namely: Duperron on the Parsis; William Jones on Sanskrit; Champollion on Ancient Egypt; Rask, the Dane, on Persia and India; and Niebuhr, Botta, Layard, and others on the Babylonian cult. It was Ernest Renan (1822-1892) who invented the term "Comparative study of religions." [20]

But in a real sense the life of Max Müller and his work marked the beginning of this new science of the History of Religions. Max Müller, born in Germany (1823), studied in Paris, and taught in London. He wrote many books, among which *Chips from a German Workshop* is best known. Finally he edited his great monument and life-work, a series of *The Sacred Books of the East*. His final theory of the origin of Religion was that the so-called original henotheistic Nature Worship degenerated into Polytheism, sank into Fetishism, and then rose in some cases to new forms of Pantheism or Theism.

Max Müller's colleague at Oxford, Tylor, followed by Andrew Lang, criticized this theory. Tylor published his book *Primitive Culture* (1871) in which he emphasized Animism as the source of all religious beliefs. This evolutionary hypothesis was eagerly welcomed by Herbert Spencer in his *Principles of Sociology* (London, 1877).

[20] According to Father Weiss, *Le Peril Religieux*. Quoted as footnote, p. 7, in Le Roy's *The Religion of the Primitives*.

Parallel with these theories Totemism came to the front. This word was first used by J. Long (1791) in reference to the beliefs of the American Indians. Frazer and Lang (for a time) followed this hypothesis, and even Robertson Smith in his *Religion of the Semites* (1889) made Totemism the most important factor in early religion. Others became their disciples, among whom were Lubbock and Jevons. This particular theory, however, did not meet with universal acceptance. A group of Dutch scholars led by Tiele (1830-1902) prepared the middle ground between the Evolution and the Revelation schools. Tiele's *Gifford Lectures on the Science of Religion* (Edinburgh, 1896) marked the new epoch. He was followed by another Hollander, P. D. Chantepie de la Saussaye (1842-1920), and by the Swiss Orelli. Neither of these writers accepted the evolutionary view; Orelli especially emphasizes the fact of primitive monotheism among all nations. The latest textbook on the History of Religions, and that which is considered the best in Germany, is based upon the work of Chantepie. The fourth edition, revised, appeared in 1925 (by Bertholet and Lehmann, Tübingen, 2 vols.).

Meanwhile, in France we find the important names of Reville, who founded a Review of the History of Religions; Darmesteter, the translator of the *Avesta;* Barth, Maspero, and Reinach. Another group of sociologists who made special study of the History of Religions was led by Durkheim. Their quarterly publications are interesting, as they frequently contain criticism of the positions taken by Tylor, Robertson Smith, etc.

The present status of the History of Religions, even among those who reject Revelation, is that neither the theory of evolution nor that of degeneration is wholly accepted other than as a hypothesis. The tendency is to deal, not with the theory of origins, but with the history of development. "Primitive Culture" no longer signifies the original condition of humanity. One hears less and less of "the noble primitive faith" of savages in their pristine innocence, because the real character of Fetishism, Magic, and Totemism is now better known. A greater emphasis was put on earlier monotheistic ideas, especially by Andrew Lang in his book *The Making of Religion* and by Howitt in *The Native Tribes of Southern Australia* (London, 1904).

Alkema and Bezemer of the University of Utrecht in their recent book *Volkenkunde van Nederlandsch Indie* have a special chapter on the origin of the Nature religions, and do not accept the evolutionary theory at all (Haarlem, 1928, pp. 126-204). They say: "The study of primitive religion has been altogether too much swayed by the evolutionary hypothesis, and those who wrote on the subject approached it with prejudgments." They give as instances Max Müller, Hegel, and Darwin, but especially Tylor (*Primitive Culture*, 1871). Wilken too followed the latter, but both were assailed by later scholarship. Many contested the conclusions reached by Tylor on the animistic origin of religion. The following may be mentioned: Mauss of Paris, Van Gennep of Neuchatel, Preusz of Berlin, Kruijt of Java, and especially Schmidt in his great work on *The Origin of the Idea of God*. In each case their conclusion is that not animistic thought, but pre-animistic knowledge of a High-god is the oldest religious conception.

The reader may, however, ask whether Dr. Schmidt speaks with authority in this realm of knowledge, or whether he is merely voicing the old orthodoxy of the Roman Catholic Church and, in this case, of evangelical Christianity. The answer is that in all of the volumes so far issued Dr. Schmidt makes no appeal to the Scriptures and (writing from the standpoint of anthropological science) gives no scriptural references. He bases his whole argument on the data gathered by scores of investigators and scholars who lived among Primitives. Father Wilhelm Schmidt is the most renowned of the group of scholars resident at St. Gabriel Scientific Institute in the suburbs of Vienna. A Westphalian, sixty-six years of age, he began to publish important studies on the South Sea languages as early as 1889. He founded *Anthropos*, the outstanding international review of ethnology and linguistics, in 1906, and was for twenty years its editor. He has written one hundred and fifty books and pamphlets on scientific subjects and is an acknowledged authority in Europe and America.[21] The only attempt I have seen to reply to his argument in *Der Ursprung*

[21] *The Catholic World*, April, 1923, gives a sketch of his work, and a *Festschrift* published in his honor (Vienna, 1928) gives a list of all his publications.

der Gottesidee is by a Dutch scholar, Dr. J. J. Fahrenfort of Gronigen University, in his book *Het Hoogste Wezen der Primitieven*.[22] He contends that the evidence for primitive monotheism given by Dr. Schmidt is inadequate and that his argument is based on presuppositions. But his thesis received a crushing reply by Dr. Schmidt in a paper published under the title "Ein Versuch zur Rettung des Evolutionismus" (An Attempt to Save Evolution) in the *International Archiv für Ethnografie* (Band XXIX, Heft VI-VI, Leiden, 1928).[23]

"Dr. Schmidt," says Bertram C. A. Windle, "is a recognized authority in ethnology; and his book, *L'Origine de l'Idee de Dieu*, is a classic on that subject. M. Mainage, another first-rate authority, summarizes his colleague's views and comes to the conclusion, as others have done, that monotheism is the primitive form of religion among all primitive races, and that we may say of the Supreme Being of such races, as both of these authors have said: 'Dieu n'est pas seulement Créateur: Il surveille et rétribue les actes des hommes, et c'est pourquoi dans l'immense majorité des cas, les lois ethniques sont référées formellement à l'Etre Suprême.' "

He goes on to say in reference to other theories for the origin of religion:

"The fact is, that all these theories suffer from this original and fatal vice—they assume a primary period of

[22] J. B. Wolters, The Hague, 1927, pp. 307.
[23] Dr. Fahrenfort replied in a pamphlet *Wie der Urmonotheismus am Leben erhalten wird* (Hagg, 1930).

atheism which is flat contrary to all the evidence. In fact, scientific anthropologists are coming back to the belief in the primary monotheism they so long scouted. Professor Swanton, for example, when delivering the Presidential Address a few years ago to the American Anthropological Association, and dealing with theories long held but now to be abandoned (such as group marriage instead of primitive monogamy which seems to have been the rule), added the statement: 'Even in the case of our regnant monotheism, it is a fair question whether it does not tie on to the belief in a sky-god extending back to the earliest days of religion among men, the only change which it has undergone being the relatively greater importance and deeper spiritualization of the concept in later times.'" [24]

Even in our own land and from unexpected quarters there are voices warning us that in the study of the History of Religions we must not neglect our principal source-book, namely, the Holy Scriptures. Professor Irving F. Wood of Smith College wrote a valuable paper on "The Contribution of the Bible to the History of Religion." His words are suggestive and make us hope for the day when Christian scholars will regard the Scriptures not only as a source-book but as "the infallible rule of faith and practice" in the comparative study of religion. Professor Wood says: [25]

"The history of Religion is the profoundest attempt to understand the inner life, the thoughts and intents of the heart, of all the peoples of the earth, ever made in the field of scholarship. The result of this has been that the Bible takes its place beside other sacred literatures as only one

[24] "The Religion of Prehistoric Man," in *The Dublin Review*, vol. clxx, 1922, pp. 170, 232.
[25] In the *Journal of Biblical Literature*, vol. 47, 1928.

of the great documents in the religious evolution of mankind. Moreover, since a knowledge of the biblical religions is often assumed—how mistakenly we all know—to be the common possession of intelligent people, the emphasis of students of the history of religion is often thrown upon those Oriental religions which require much explanation if they are to be understood by Occidentals; or even upon the religious ideas and practices of primitive races.

"So far has the pendulum swung in this direction that the student of the Bible sometimes seems to be the acolyte at a minor shrine in the great temple where are placed the altars of the religions of the world. It is time for the pendulum to swing back somewhat. Bible students may well claim the supremacy of the Bible among the literary sources of the History of Religion; not on the old ground that it presents the true religion and all the rest are false, but on the ground that it is the literature of greatest importance. It presents much material in better form than any other literature; and it presents some supremely important elements not presented at all elsewhere."

Professor Wood does not go far enough, and yet we are grateful. He gives as reasons for his position that: (1) Other Sacred Scriptures are detached from history while the Bible is embedded in history; (2) for the most part the literature of the great Oriental religions is in a social vacuum, but the Bible gives the religious biography of a nation; (3) the Bible is the one book where we can clearly trace the growth of an ethical monotheism. And he concludes:

"The Bible does not philosophize, yet the most important contributions in that field will come, I am confident, from the familiar pages of the Bible. Biblical scholarship will yet bear the leading part in the history of religion."

If this is true, it is evident that we cannot wholly discard such a book as the Bible, whatever its origin, in the study of the origin of religion and its various elements.

The knowledge of other religions undoubtedly is valuable to the missionary who is anxious to find points of contact between himself and the non-Christian world, valuable for comparative purposes, to show wherein Christianity excels all other religions, valuable also as showing that these religions were providential anticipations of a wider and more important truth; but most of all valuable because it creates a spirit of sympathy and "compassion for the ignorant and those that are out of the way." This is indispensable to everyone who would have the heart and mind of Jesus Christ.

For, as Dr. Oesterly points out:

"The study of Comparative Religion will in the future become one of the greatest dangers to the Christian religion, or else its handmaiden. If the former, then Christian Apologetics will have to find new defensive armour; but if the latter, then its offensive armour will have become stronger than ever." [26]

The missionary enterprise is to make disciples of all nations for Christ, not merely to share our own experiences with those of other faiths. The Jerusalem Council message in 1928 asserted unequivocally and without compromise the finality and absoluteness of Jesus Christ and at the same time insisted that we are

[26] L. H. Jordan, *Comparative Religion: A Survey of Its Literature*, London, 1920, p. 91.

HISTORY OF ORIGINS IN RELIGION

to find avenues of approach and points of contact with those of other faiths by a thorough and sympathetic study of what is best in their creeds and conduct. Only by such scholarly effort and painstaking approach can we learn the values of the non-Christian religions and the value of those values.[27]

Moreover, this branch of learning is of use not only to the future missionary, but to every earnest student, because the eye that has been sharpened through a comparative study of religions can better realize the religious content of Christianity itself; and the history of Christianity can be rightly understood only when one has studied the non-Christian religions which have borrowed so much and from which Christianity has borrowed so little; and above all, to which it stands in sharp contrast as the religion of Revelation and Redemption.[28]

No one can ignore the science of the History of Religions. It is found in popular form in our best magazines and in all sorts of handbooks (some of them superficial and a few even supercilious) which profess to introduce the West to the philosophies of the East. In any case, for better or for worse, the comparative study of religion and the history of re-

[27] Report of the Jerusalem Meeting, vol. i, pp. 341-459.

[28] "We must strive to understand and explain the other religions from the standpoint of Christianity. Too often the reverse has been the case. While it is true that the natural is first and then the spiritual, it is also true, as Paul says, that the spiritual man discerneth all things." Chantepie de la Saussaye, *Die Vergleichende Religions-forschung und der Religiöse Glaube* (Frieburg, 1898), p. 25.

ligion is now carried on in our colleges and universities, not to speak of high schools, and the problems that it raises must be solved by facing them squarely, not by ignoring them. The depreciation of the Old Testament and the exaltation of the Sacred Books of other faiths have sometimes gone hand in hand. Christ's words, "I came not to destroy but to fulfil," have been wrested out of their context and made to mean that he came to fulfil the Bhagavad-gita, the Analects of Confucius, and even the Koran! while the Old Testament is designated "mere folklore" and so often goes by the board. It is highly encouraging that, in contrast to this easy-going anti-supernaturalistic tendency, we have the works of Andrew Lang,[29] von Orelli,[30] S. H. Kellogg,[31] and Pettazoni,[32] not to mention St. Clair Tisdall, Jevons, and others. At the conclusion of his study of *The Religion of the Primitives*, Le Roy comes to a rather conservative value-judgment, which will be confirmed by what follows in our discussion:

"In this great question [of the origin of religion] as it presents itself to us, the human species migrated from the original spot where it first appeared, at a period which science is powerless to determine in a precise manner. There had been put into its possession a fund of religious and moral truths, with the elements of a worship, the whole rooted in the very nature of man, and there conserved

[29] *The Making of Religion.*
[30] *Allgemeine Religionsgeschichte.*
[31] *The Genesis and Growth of Religion.*
[32] "La Formation du Monotheisme" in *Revue de l'Histoire des Religions*, vol. 88, pp. 193-229, Paris, 1923.

HISTORY OF ORIGINS IN RELIGION

along with the family, developing with society. Each race, according to its particular mentalities, its intellectual tendency, and the special conditions of its life, gradually established those superficially varied but fundamentally identical forms that we call religions. Everywhere and from the beginning, there were attached to these religions myths, superstitions, and magics which vitiated and disfigured them and turned them from their object." [33]

Stephen H. Langdon of Oxford comes to a like conclusion in his book on *Semitic Mythology,* as already quoted in our introduction.[34]

In the chapters that follow we deal primarily with "primitive religion" so-called or, better, the religious beliefs and practices of primitive tribes in the earlier stages of culture. But we cannot wholly ignore the great ethnic faiths of historic origin. Here too the roots of religion go back to prehistoric time. Do they show signs of progressive evolution or of deterioration?

Four of the great living non-Christian religions today are Judaism, Hinduism, Buddhism, and Islam. The strength of these systems of thought lies not in their bad qualities or tendencies, but in their good; not in their erroneous teachings, but in their truths and half-truths. To study them with sympathy, therefore, we must seek to know what was their origin, where their strength lies today, and what are the elements of truth and beauty in them.

[33] *The Religion of the Primitives,* p. 319.
[34] *The Mythology of All Races,* London, 1931, vol. 5, *Semitic,* pp. xviii, 93.

Now the central affirmation of Hinduism is in its pantheistic formula "Thou art that";[35] the personal becomes the impersonal, and the denial of personality in God and man issues in a pantheism in which moral distinctions tend completely to disappear by an overemphasis of the truth of God's immanence. The central affirmation of Buddhism is that the renunciation of desire, even the desire to live, is the way of escape from the misery of existence. It is an overemphasis of the truth of death-to-self and of man's nothingness. The central affirmation of Mohammedanism is the absolute unity of God and his sovereignty, the Pantheism of Force, an overemphasis of God's transcendence and a denial of his Incarnation. The central thought of Judaism is the holiness of God and his covenant faithfulness to a chosen people; although the rejection of the Messiah resulted in an arrested development and confined the program of the race to Zionism.

The central affirmation of the Christian religion is that God, who is eternally both transcendent and immanent, became incarnate in Christ, taking sinful man back into his favor and that by his death and resurrection we have redemption through his blood and receive, by grace alone, forgiveness of sin and eternal life and joy—and are translated from bondage into the glorious liberty of the sons of God, to share with

---

[35] "The whole doctrine of the Vedanta is summed up in two Upanishadic phrases: *Verily One without second,* and *Thou art that.* There exists nothing but absolute thought, Self, Brahma." Barnett's *Bhagavad-gita,* p. 27.

him the unspeakable privilege of extending his kingdom among men.

Now in trying to present this unique message, contact with non-Christian thought and life often sheds light on the vital elements of Christianity, deepens our conception of its truths, and brings out forgotten or underestimated doctrines. Against the darkness or twilight-shadows of heathenism and Islam, Christian beliefs and ideas are thrown into bold relief, like a sunlit face in one of Rembrandt's paintings.

This applies to such doctrines as Inspiration and Revelation when compared with the Islamic idea; the Virgin birth when compared with so-called parallels in other religions; the Trinity; the Atonement; Predestination according to Paul and according to Islamic theology; the immortality of the soul and the resurrection of the body in contrast with the Hindu belief in metempsychosis or an infinite series of incarnations; the life of the believer hid in Christ with the Hindu doctrine of *Bhakti*.

The life and history of Islam, for example, afford the strongest psychological argument and historical proof of the irrepressible yearning of the heart for a divine-human mediator. For the religion that came to stamp out the deification of Christ ended in an apotheosis of its own prophet, Mohammed, and even in almost universal saint-worship. Gottfried Simon testifies that his study of Islam in Sumatra deepened his appreciation of vital Christianity. "Certain aspects of Christian doctrine which seemed to me not fundamental for my own religious life have been shown by comparison with Islam to be indispensable and constructive elements." [36] And Canon Geoffrey Dale of Zanzibar says that, in contact with Islam, Christians are compelled to think through the exact meaning of their belief in the unity of God and forced to apprehend more clearly the idea of the transcendence of God when "they have been startled into self-examination by the *in-sha-Allah* and the *Alhamdu-'lillah* of the Moslem." [37]

Also, face to face with non-Christians, we will learn to use simpler and less confusing spiritual terminology and see to it that the Christian message is clad in a garb that will do it no discredit. At some of the conferences we held in South India in 1928, it was resolved that "the Indian Church should set apart some of its members for definite Christian work among Moslems, for this would help to clarify and crystallize the theology and strengthen the life of the South Indian Church." It was a Moslem theologian, Ibn-al-Arabi, who said "that the error of Christianity does not lie in making Christ God, but that it lies in making God Christ." [38] What did he mean? The depth of the riches both of the wisdom and knowledge of God as revealed in the doctrine of the Holy Trinity becomes more real and precious when we are compelled by Moslem thought to take it out of the category of mere

[36] *Vital Forces of Christianity and Islam*, p. 121.
[37] *Ibid.*, p. 210.
[38] *Ibid.*, p. 190.

dogma into the realm of vital Christian experience. When we see an intellectual stumblingblock become a stepping-stone to faith and joy and the abundant life in Moslem converts, then we realize that the Trinity is the very heart of Christian theism.[39] On the other hand, as the late Canon Temple Gairdner reminds us, "The Unity of God needs to be emphasized afresh. Some presentations of the Atonement that were distressingly suggestive of Tri-theism, even to the extent of asserting the existence of differences of ethical character within the Godhead, may be henceforth buried, surely unlamented." [40]

The greatest gain of all from a true and sympathetic study of the History of Religion will be the conviction of the finality and sufficiency of Christ. This is foreshadowed in the Old Testament. It is remarkable how many of the ancient heathen religions are referred to in the Bible. Every careful reader notices the number and variety of the forms of idolatry with which Israel came into contact: Babylonian, Assyrian, Egyptian, Phoenician, Moabite, Ammonite, Hittite, Philistinian, Greek, and Roman cults and deities—"gods many and lords many." Yet in the midst of such an environment the universal mission and message of Israel to the nations was never lost from sight. The unity of the race, the fatherhood of God, the promise of blessing to Noah, and for all nations of the earth through Abraham's seed in the fulness of time; the

[39] Zwemer, *The Moslem Doctrine of God*, pp. 107-120.
[40] *Vital Forces of Christianity and Islam*, p. 38.

prophecies of Isaiah, Amos, Habakkuk, Jeremiah, Ezekiel, Daniel, Joel, Haggai, and Malachi concerning the Messiah, all proclaim that the name of Jehovah "shall be great from the rising of the sun to the going down of the same" and that this knowledge shall once "cover the whole earth as the waters cover the sea." Only one Savior, only one Servant of Jehovah, only one name exalted above every name, only one Messiah, only one son-of-man sitting on the throne of judgment, only one kingdom that is to be established forever when the kingdoms of this world have become the kingdom of the Lord of his Christ.

The New Testament has the same universal outlook and the same emphasis of one, only Savior. Our Lord himself and his apostles were conscious of a world mission. Although he was sent primarily to the lost sheep of the house of Israel, he is the Good Shepherd who has other sheep among all nations. Although Von Harnack (in a chapter which Dr. James Moffatt characterized as the most controversial and the least convincing of his great work on *The Mission and Expansion of Christendom*) concludes that Jesus was *not* conscious of a universal mission and that the great commission as recorded is *not* genuine; yet, in that very chapter Harnack admits that the fourth gospel is saturated with statements of a directly universalistic character. And he concludes that "Christ shattered Judaism and brought out the kernel of the religion of

HISTORY OF ORIGINS IN RELIGION

Israel, thereby, and by his own death founded the universal religion." [41]

The universality and finality of the Christian Revelation of God in Christ has been maintained on various grounds, scriptural, ethical, philosophical, or for missionary, that is to say, pragmatic reasons. Dr. Heinrich Frick argued that "we do not need a new interpretation of Christian missions, but rather a revival of their most ancient form based on the consciousness of the final and absolute superiority of the Gospel over all the other religious messages of the world." [42] A thoughtful writer of the Anglican Church based a strong argument for the finality and absoluteness of Christianity on the sole fact of the Incarnation and its implications. [43]

The miracle of History, the miracle above all miracles, is Jesus Christ, who was born of the Virgin, who died on the Cross, and who is alive forevermore. Those who have experienced his love and forgiveness never doubt that he is the only and sufficient Savior. For them the two eternities, past and future, and the whole period lying in between are united and controlled by one purpose, redemption through Christ. He is the Alpha and the Omega. In all things he has the pre-eminence. He will yet reconcile all things unto

[41] *The Mission and Expansion of Christianity*, vol. i, chap. iv. Cf. the very able reply of Max Meinertz, *Jesus und die Heidenmission*, Münster, 1925.

[42] Article in *International Review of Missions*, "Is a Conviction of the Superiority of His Message Essential to the Missionary?"

[43] Rev. J. K. Mozley in *The Church Overseas*, January, 1930.

himself, whether things upon the earth or things in the Heavens. He will restore the lost harmony of the universe, because to him every knee shall bow and every tongue confess. This is the glorious and certain goal of the long history of religions and of the yet unfinished task of missions.

CHAPTER TWO

THE ORIGIN OF RELIGION

"THE scene today is entirely different from what it was in the time of Victoria. Then evolution, with its implicit doctrine of the perfectibility of man by his own inherent virtues, combined with the extraordinary mechanical and industrial development of the age and the far-reaching discoveries of the scientists to produce an illusion of the inevitability of progress. More than one of these essays summarize the steady disillusionment of our own time until so far from expecting the announcement of the inauguration of Utopia many men have ceased to believe in the future of European civilization. The fundamental ground upon which humanism was negativing Christianity, that man had risen from the dust and was rapidly approaching perfection, has proved mere marshland, and the structure reared upon it has fallen. Earlier in the century Bernard Shaw had doubted whether man could solve the problems that his own civilization had created; and today the atmosphere of disillusionment, of suspecting that there may be something amiss not only with material civilization but with man himself, provides a better opportunity for orthodoxy to state its case than it has had for many generations."

THE LONDON TIMES
in a review of Sidney Dark's
Orthodoxy Sees It Through,
June 28, 1934.

CHAPTER TWO

THE ORIGIN OF RELIGION
BY EVOLUTION OR BY REVELATION

IN THE SIXTEENTH EDITION OF A POPULAR ACCOUNT of the great religions of mankind, Lewis Browne relates in the prologue how he thinks it all began:

"In the beginning there was fear; and fear was in the heart of man; and fear controlled man. At every turn it whelmed over him, leaving him no moment of ease. With the wild soughing of the wind it swept through him; with the crashing of the thunder and the growling of lurking beasts. All the days of man were gray with fear, because all his universe seemed charged with danger. . . . And he, poor gibbering half-ape, nursing his wound in some draughty cave, could only tremble with fear."[1]

The evolutionary hypothesis seems to have the right of way, not only in such popular works by non-Christians, but with Christian writers as well. We quote from two recent works on the study of the history of religion:

"There was a belief once that religion began with a full knowledge of one true God and that thereafter through human fault and disobedience the light of the first splendid

[1] *This Believing World,* 16th edition, p. 5.

vision was clouded or lost. But this is not the story told by the assembled records. The story of religion is not a recessional. The worship of sticks and stones is not religion fallen into the dark; it is religion rising out of the dark. The procession of the gods has been an advance and not a retreat. The faiths of the dark and the dawn are not 'a sleep and a forgetting'; they are man's religious awakening and his first suppliant gesture toward the unseen. Why did he make this gesture?" [2]

Professor E. D. Soper in his *Religions of Mankind* puts it even more frankly:

"Christians, Jews, and Mohammedans alike assumed a primitive divine revelation, and that settled the whole question. They conceived that in the beginning—that means when the first man was created and placed in the Garden of Eden—God revealed to him in some manner the essential truths of religion, such as the existence of one God, the obligation to obey him, and the hope of immortality. Thus furnished, he began his career, but when sin emerged the revelation became hazy and indistinct and finally was well-nigh if not completely lost. The difficulty with this exceedingly fascinating picture is that it rests on no solid foundation of fact. The Bible makes no clear statement which would lead to this conclusion. When man began to play his part he performed religious acts and engaged at times in a religious ritual; so much is evident, but nothing is said as to origins. That man received his religious nature from God is very plausible, but that differs widely from the statement that he came into life furnished with a full set of religious ideas. The theory of evolution presents us with a very different account of early man, an account which makes belief in a more or less complete revelation incongruous." [3]

[2] Professor G. G. Atkins, *Procession of the Gods*, p. 5.
[3] Professor E. D. Soper, *Religions of Mankind*, pp. 29, 30.

According to writers of this school, the Hebrew religion itself is largely due to a process of evolution. Yahweh was from time immemorial the tribal god of the Midianites and his abode was Mount Sinai. From the Kenite priest Jethro, Moses gained the knowledge of Yahweh. So the later covenant at Sinai is presented in the form that Israel chose Yahweh, not that Yahweh chose Israel. Volcanic phenomena account for the terrors at the giving of the Law. There was an ancient pastoral feast called Passover, and it is not impossible that a form of the seventh day Sabbath was imposed. "Beyond these points it is hardly possible even to hazard a conjecture." Later on, much later on, the prophets proclaimed a higher conception of deity as Lord of all and a universal morality.[4] Here again we have the hypothesis of evolution applied to the documents and teachings of the Old Testament, and the argument has become familiar.

But the verdict is not unanimous. In a recent important work by Dr. Israel Rabin, entitled *Studien zur Vormosaischen Gottesvorstellung,* this orthodox Jew protests against the view that monotheism was a later development in Israel and that it was preceded by polytheism and animism. Not only Moses, he says, but the Patriarchs were already monotheists. "The Covenant idea is as old as Abraham, and the covenant at Sinai

---

[4] W. O. E. Oesterley and Theodore Robinson, *Hebrew Religion: Its Origin and Development,* pp. 4-16, 22, 23, 175, etc. For a contrary view see Adolf Loods, "Le monotheisme a-t-il eu des précurseurs parmi les Sages de l'ancien Orient?" in *Revue d'histoire et de philosophie religieuse,* June, 1934.

is history, not fiction. The God of Sinai is no mere mountain-god or local Kenite god. Monotheism is not the result of an evolutionary process, but it rests upon revelation and existed from the beginning of Israel's history as portrayed in Genesis; there is no bridge from polytheism to monotheism." There is no bridge from polytheism to monotheism unless it be one-way traffic across the chasm in the other direction.

In the history of religion and in the study of the origin of the idea of God the neglected factors are coming to their own. Entirely apart from the teaching of the early chapters in Genesis and Paul's statement in the first chapter of Romans, the evidence for primitive High-gods and for early monotheism in the ethnic religions can no longer be ignored. Recent scholarship on both sides of the Atlantic agrees that not evolution but innate knowlege or a revelation is the key to the origin of the idea of God, of immortality, and of the rites of prayer and sacrifice. This we shall see later on.

The first modern writer to emphasize the fact that monotheistic ideas were found among primitive races and must be taken into account was Andrew Lang in his book *The Making of Religion* (1898).[5] In 1924 Redan delivered an address before the Jewish Historical Society on *Monotheism among Primitive Peoples*, in which he wholly rejected the evolutionary hypothesis. "Most of us," said he, "have been brought up in

[5] Andrew Lang, *The Making of Religion*, London, pp. 173-209. Cf. our next chapter for summary of the book.

or influenced by the tenets of orthodox ethnology, and this was largely an enthusiastic and quite uncritical attempt to apply the Darwinian theory of evolution to the facts of social experience. Many ethnologists, sociologists, and psychologists still persist in this endeavor. No progress will ever be achieved, however, until scholars rid themselves, once and for all, of the curious notion that everything possesses an evolutionary history; until they realize that certain ideas and certain concepts are as ultimate for man as a social being as specific physiological reactions are for him as a biological entity."

It is encouraging to note that the tide has turned and that we have, especially on the European Continent, outstanding scholars in this field who hold fast to supernaturalism and are opposed to the evolutionary hypothesis as the sole key to the history of religion. Among them we may mention the late Archbishop Söderblom of Sweden, Alfred Bertholet and Edward Blum-Ernst, Le Roy, Albert C. Kruijt, but especially P. Wilhelm Schmidt, founder of the anthropological review *Anthropos* and Professor of Ethnology and Philology in the University of Vienna. The exhaustive work of this Roman Catholic savant on the origin of the idea of God, *Der Ursprung der Gottesidee,* is to be completed in six massive volumes. In the five which have already appeared, he weighs in the balance the various theories of Lubbock, Spencer, Tylor, Andrew Lang, Frazer, and others, and finds them all wanting. The idea of God, he concludes, did not come by evolution but by revelation, and the evidence, massed together, analyzed, and sifted with scholarly acumen, is altogether convincing.

In 1934, Dr. K. L. Bellon, Professor in the University of Nymegen, published an introduction to the science of comparative religion, in the Holland language, in which he follows the general outline of Professor Schmidt, with whose conclusions he seems to be in thorough agreement:

"As a positive result of the investigation of P. W. Schmidt, we must undoubtedly accept that the oldest cultures and the most primitive tribes have knowledge of an almighty and beneficent High-god. How this belief originated we do not know, but we do know with certainty that it did not originate from any of the factors or germs proposed in evolutionary theories, because this belief in a High-god is rooted in the noblest faculties of man, namely his mind, and emotions, and his will, even among the most primitive tribes." [6]

Dr. Frederick Schleiter in his book, *Religion and Culture* (New York, 1919), also opposes the evolutionary theory because

"All evolutionary schemes of religion, without exception, in the determination of the primordium and the serial stages of alleged development, proceed upon a purely arbitrary and uncontrolled basis; in this manner, from a primary point of orientation, they are indefinitely numerous, and, if we spread before ourselves dispassionately a number of classical evolutionary schemes, there is little

---

[6] *Inleiding tot de Vergelijkende Godsdientwetenschap* (1934), p. 380.

THE ORIGIN OF RELIGION

reason to accord preferential respectability to any one of them on the ground of a relatively greater degree of plausibility." (p. 39.)

Earlier in this volume he expresses himself still more forcibly.

"One of the dogmas which has been very popular with evolutionary writers from time immemorial, is that the idea of God is a relatively late development in history and represents a mature flowering, as it were, of the religious spirit which is immanent in man. Investigation, however, entirely fails to support this view, there being considerable evidence that the concept of an omnipotent being may arise spontaneously among the most primitive tribes." (p. 35.)

Anthropology and ethnology are also swinging away from the old evolutionary concept as regards primitive races. Dr. Robert H. Lowie of the American Museum of Natural History, in his recent important study on *Primitive Society*, says:

"The time has come for eschewing the all-embracing and baseless theories of yore to settle down to sober historical research. The Africans did not pass from a Stone Age to an Age of Copper and Bronze and then to an Iron Age . . . . they passed directly from stone tools to the manufacture of iron tools."[7]

He concludes that "neither morphologically nor dynamically can social life be said to have progressed from a stage of savagery to a stage of enlightenment." Whatever may be the reaction of students of anthropology to a doctrine so alien to tradition still prevail-

[7] Dr. Robert H. Lowie, *Primitive Society*, 13th edition, New York, pp. 436, 437.

ing among many scholars, it will do no harm to face the arguments here presented with such force and apparently so well documented. The *London Times Literary Supplement,* in reviewing Schmidt's book at considerable length, did so under the title *Evolution or Eden.* It is inevitable that Dr. Schmidt divides investigators of the history of religion into two classes— the believing and the unbelieving. By the latter he means those scholars who have themselves repudiated all faith in the supernatural, and "will talk of religion as a blind man might of colors, or one totally devoid of hearing of a beautiful musical composition." [8]

The work is divided into five parts. The introduction deals with the nature, aim, and method of comparative study of religion and the history of the subject. Part Two sketches the theories that were in vogue during the nineteenth century, namely those that found the origin of religion in Nature-myths, Fetishism, Manism or Ghost-worship, and animism. Part Three deals with the twentieth century, and sketches the Pan-Babylonian theory, Totemism, Magianism, and Dynamism. In every case Dr. Schmidt gives an exposition of these various theories and a refutation of them based upon more accurate data from later investigations.

One can give in a table the outstanding theories of the origin of religion together with their leading advo-

[8] *The Origin and Growth of Religion: Facts and Theories,* by W. Schmidt. Translated by H. J. Rose. The Dial Press, New York, 1931, p. 297.

cates and the element of truth emphasized in regard to primitive beliefs, as follows:

1. Nature myths—Max Muller—Immanence of the supernatural.
2. Fetishism—Lubbock—Awe for the supernatural.
3. Manism—Herbert Spencer—Immortality of the soul.
4. Animism—Tylor—The super-sensuous in all creation.
5. Star myths—Jeremias—Transcendence.
6. Totemism—Frazer—Exogamy in family-life.
7. Magism—King and Durkheim—Sacramental idea.
8. Sky-gods—Lang—Creation.
9. Primitive High-god—Schmidt—Revelation.

Of all these theories, only the fourth has large following today among those who reject the findings of Andrew Lang and Wilhelm Schmidt. The full evidence is found in the encyclopedic work of the latter, *Der Ursprung der Gottesidee* (in seven volumes) and in his English books, *The Origin and Growth of Religion*.

In Part Four we have an account of the supreme Sky-gods whose existence was posited by Andrew Lang and others. It appears that during the twentieth century there was a progressive recognition of the primitive High-god by European and American students of ethnology and religion. This protest against the evolutionary theory applies not only to the religion of primitives, but to those who find the same development in the religion of the Old Testament.

Dr. Schmidt follows the historical method mentioned in our first chapter, and traces the belief in a supreme God across the wide areas where primitive culture prevails; for example, among the Pygmies of Africa, the Indians of North America, and certain tribes in Australia. The last chapter of this epoch-making book is entitled "The Origin and History of the Primitive High-god," in which we have the summary of the argument.

"That the Supreme Being of the primitive culture is really the god of a monotheism, and that the religion which includes him is genuinely monotheistic—this is the position which is most attacked by a number of authors. To this attack we may reply that there is a sufficient number of tribes among whom the really monotheistic character of their Supreme Being is clear even to a cursory examination. That is true of the Supreme Being of most Pygmy tribes, so far as we know them; also of the Tierra del Fuegians, the primitive Bushmen, the Kurnai, Kulin, and Yuin of Southeast Australia, the peoples of the Arctic culture, except the Koryaks, and well-nigh all the primitives of North America."

Again, in massing the evidence for the character of this Supreme Being, he says:

"The name 'father' is applied to the Supreme Being in every single area of the primitive culture when he is addressed or appealed to. It seems, therefore, that we may consider it primeval and proper to the oldest primitive culture. We find it in the form 'father' simply, also in the individual form ('my father') and the collective ('our father'). So far, this name has not been discovered among the Central African Pygmies, but it exists among the Bushmen and the Mountain Dama. It is lacking also among the Andamanese and the Philippine Negritos, but is found, although not commonly, among the Semang. Among the Samoyeds we find the formula 'my Num-father,' i.e., sky-father. In North Central California, the name occurs among the Pomo and the Patwin; all three forms of it are widely distributed among the Algonkians. It is also widely current among the two oldest Tierra del Fuegian tribes, the Yamana and the Halakwulup, who use the form 'my father.' Among all the tribes of Southeast Australia it is in common use in the form 'our father.' There it is the oldest name of all, and even the women and children know it; the oldest of the tribes, the Kurnai, have no other name for Him. There is no doubt possible that the name 'father' is intended in this connection to denote, not psysiological paternity (save in cases where the figures of the Supreme Being and of the First Father have coalesced), but an attitude of the greatest reverence, of tender affection and steadfast trust on the part of man toward his god."

The evidence for these astonishing statements is abundantly given in the larger six-volume work, to which we have already referred. In his lectures on *High-gods in North America,* given at Oxford last year, Dr. Schmidt gives further evidence for his view that the gods of these tribes were true gods with moral attributes, and that their beliefs possess a high religious value. Incidentally he proves that this pure religious faith comes before fetishism, animism, ghost-worship, totemism, or magism, from one or another of which evolution theories had derived the origin of religion. The Professor claims to have made it clear by his discoveries that "progressive evolution is not the key which opens the door to a true history of humanity, and consequently of man's religion." The peoples ethnologically oldest know nothing of totemism or any similar phenomena, but emphasize in their religion the creative power of the Supreme Being. Not evolution, but degeneration or deterioration, is found in the history of religion among primitive tribes and the higher cultures that followed after their migration.

In the same series of lectures Professor Schmidt, after reviewing all the evidence in the case of three groups of Indians, states:

"In each of these religions there exists a true High-god: nay, I do not hesitate to employ a more decided phrase and say: 'These people worship One God.' Sometime ago Archbishop Söderblom refused to recognize these High-gods as more than 'originators' (Urheber), and said, with a tinge of irony, that such an 'originator' was neither 'one' nor 'God'; but I hope I have now shown him to be really both. A High-god of this type is *one,* for in his oldest and most original form he has beside him no figures of animistic or manistic type to prejudice his absolute supremacy; in particular, he has neither wife nor child. . . .

"Thus we have in those religions a true God who is truly one; not a distant, cold 'originator,' but a true Supreme God, who is not afar off; not a stranger to men, but one who takes a keen interest in and exercises manifold influences on their life; whom also men do not consider as a stranger, but to whom they address themselves in a lively worship comprising a variety of prayers, sacrifices, and ceremonies. Quite remarkable is the wide diffusion of

THE ORIGIN OF RELIGION

prayer, which we encountered so frequently at morning, evening, and mealtimes. Not less astonishing is the frequency of true offerings of first-fruits, by which the supreme power of the Creator and Master of life and death is so simply and so solemnly recognized." [9]

In a recent book by Marc Boegner with the startling title, *God, the Eternal Torment of Man,* there are also some interesting references to the High-gods among primitive races. He says:

"The heathen, of whom we often speak much but know little, experience this torment of separation from God. The missionary Rusillon, who has made a most useful study of the Negroes, shows in a recent book on heathenism that they understand what separates them from God. They themselves are to blame. Their legends say so without evasion. 'Even today the heathen soul accuses itself all through its stories, legends, and proverbs. If it is separated from God as a result of its own voluntary act, it has seriously offended him. The responsibility for the rupture reverts to man, and he has never discovered the way to bring God back. In consequence he has deep in his heart a profound homesick longing.' " [10]

Again in these same lectures, given in Paris, the same writer speaks of the retrogression in religion as follows:

"We have noted in our survey of the world of the gods the very opposite of progressions, what we can call *digressions*. For example, this change, so characteristic, from a monotheism which appeared primitive—to the extent that we can speak of primitive—to distinctly inferior forms of religious life. How is this to be accounted for from the

[9] Pp. 129, 131.
[10] P. 23.

point of view of *sociologisme?* 'The language of the heathen of the present day,' the missionary Rusillon points out, is 'chock-full of ideas which they have forgotten and is better than their heart.' "[11]

The most recent testimony in corroboration of Schmidt's theory is that given by the French scholar who wrote on *The Conversion of Primitives,* and to whom Boegner refers, as follows:

"What conclusion is to be reached, gentlemen, on this matter, except that the problem of primitive monotheism which would be found at the source of human beliefs is far from being solved? Raoul Allier indicates this most judiciously in a very important note to his book: 'When we took up our task,' he says, 'this idea of a primitive monotheism appeared to us inspired by an *a priori* dogmatism. The investigations of Pere W. Schmidt (a Catholic scholar, universally known and respected) now appear to us disquieting. . . . The notion of a Supreme Being gives the impression now and again of becoming more clearly defined the farther back through the course of the ages we go. It is recognized that scholars, and not the least of them, are declaring today that the whole problem must be taken up again.' "

Père H. M. Dubois, who has made special study of the religions of Madagascar, finds here also a substratum of belief in a Supreme God back of all animistic and manistic conceptions. "The authentic names of his High-god in ancient Malagasy are Andriamanitra and Zanahary." He gives evidence that between

[11] Pp. 49, 50.

Zanahary and the Manes (spirits) there is a vast difference as regards attributes and worship.[12]

It is clear that Dr. Schmidt is not the first or only authority on primitive monotheism over against other theories for the origin of religion. Fifty years ago Dr. Francis L. Patton summed up the argument for his day:

"It is more important to note the fact, that aside from the declarations of Scripture upon the subject, there is good reason to believe that Monotheism was the primitive religion. And it is certainly true that polytheism, fetishism, and idolatry are corruptions of an earlier and purer faith. 'Five thousand years ago the Chinese were monotheists—not henotheists, but monotheists; and this monotheism was in danger of being corrupted, as we have seen, by a nature-worship on the one hand, and by a system of superstitious divination on the other.' So says Dr. Legge. And says M. Emmanuel Rouge: 'The first characteristic of the religion of ancient Egypt is the unity of God, most energetically expressed.' Says LePage Renouf: 'The gods of the Egyptian, as well as those of the Indian, Greek, or Teutonic mythologies, were the "powers" of nature, the "strong ones," whose might was seen and felt to be irresistible, yet so constant, unchanging, and orderly in its operations, as to leave no doubt as to the presence of an ever-living and active intelligence.' Says Professor Grimm: 'The monotheistic form appears to be the more ancient, and that out of which antiquity in its infancy formed polytheism.' . . . All mythologies lead us to this conclusion.' This, too, was once the belief of Max Müller, though, as has been shown, his opinions seem to have undergone a change under the pressure of a demand that

[12] H. M. Dubois, "L'idée de Dieu chez les anciens Malgaches," in *Anthropos*, xxiv, pp. 281-311, and xxix, pp. 757-774.

religion shall be accounted for as a product of man's five senses. 'The more we go back, the more explain the earliest germs of any religion, the purer, I believe, we shall find the conceptions of the Deity, the nobler the purposes of each founder of a new worship." [13]

The fact is that the evolutionary theory as an explanation of the history of religion is more and more being abandoned. It has raised more difficulties than it has explained. Professor Dr. J. Huizenga of Utrecht University gave an address a few years ago on the history of human culture in which he actually defended this thesis: "The evolutionary theory has been a liability and not an asset in the scientific treatment of the history of civilization." [14]

The degeneration theory (that is, in scriptural language, sin and the fall of man) is gaining adherents among enthnologists who are not theologians. Among them is R. R. Marett, who speaks of ups and downs in the history of religion and whose recent lectures on *Faith, Hope, and Charity in Primitive Religion* (New York, 1932) are the very opposite of proof for the evolution of the religious idea. Not only was incest a crime, but monogamy was the earliest form of marriage among the most primitive tribes. Primitive man believed in immortality and, after a fashion, in a world beyond. "Neanderthal man, to whom we grudge the name of *homo sapiens*," says Marett, "achieved a future

[13] "The Origin of Theism," *Presbyterian Review*, October, 1882.
[14] Quoted in Alkema and Bezemer's *Volkenkunde van Nederlandsch Indie* (Haarlem, 1927), p. 134. Cf. the entire chapter on "Degeneration" in this important work on primitive tribes of the Dutch East Indies.

life. There can be no question, I think, that the experts are right in attributing to him deliberate burials with due provision for a hereafter. It is even noticeable that funeral custom is already beyond its earliest stage. At La Chapelle-aux-Saints, for instance, not only is the grave neatly dug and food laid by conveniently, but a cave too small for habitation has evidently been selected for a purely sepulchral purpose. If there was a time when the dead man was simply left lying by himself within his own cave-home, or when, perhaps, the dying man was prematurely abandoned, we are well past it." [15]

Dr. Carl Clemen also finds evidence for religion during the paleolithic period such as belief in a future life, sacrifice, etc.,[16] while in his latest book on *The Fear of the Dead in Primitive Religion,* Sir James G. Frazer uses these remarkable words:

"Men commonly believe that their conscious being will not end at death, but that it will be continued for an indefinite time or forever, long after the frail corporeal envelope which lodged it for a time has moldered in the dust. This belief in the immortality of the soul, as we call it, is by no means confined to the adherents of those great historical religions which are now professed by the most

[15] P. 34.

[16] *Urgeschichtliche Religion,* Bonn, 1932. "The importance of these discoveries in their effect on modern beliefs and on contemporary literature cannot be overestimated. They transcend in importance Einstein's discovery of Relativity. What skyscrapers of erudition have been erected on the assumption, expressed or implied, of the evolution of religion! And now the time has come when they prove to be unsound at their very foundation!"—Sir Charles Marston, F.S.A., in a paper read at the Victoria Institute, London, April, 1934.

civilized nations of the world; it is held with at least equal confidence by most, if not all, of those peoples of lower culture whom we call savages or barbarians, and there is every reason to think that among them the belief is native; in other words, that it originated among them in a stage of savagery at least as low as that which they now occupy, and that it has been handed down among them from generation to generation without being materially modified by contact with races at higher levels of culture. It is therefore a mistake to suppose that the hope of immortality after death was first revealed to mankind by the founders of the great historical religions, Buddhism, Christianity, and Islam; to all appearance, it was cherished by men all over the world thousands of years before Buddha, Jesus Christ, and Mohammed were born."

If we have belief in immortality, faith, hope, and love, knowledge of a High-god or Sky-god and conscience with its taboos and dread of judgment, how does *that* kind of primitive man of ethnology differ psychologically from Adam in the Book of Genesis?

Professor Le Roy, after twenty years among the tribes of Africa, states that "when you have lived with primitives a long time, when you have come to be accepted as one of them, entering into their life and mentality, and are acquainted with their language, practices, and beliefs, you reach the conclusion that behind what is called their naturism, animism, or fetishism, everywhere there rises up real and living, though often more or less veiled, the notion of a higher God, above men, manes, spirits, and all the forces of nature. Other beliefs are variable, like the ceremonies attached to them, but this one is universal and fundamental." [17]

Schmidt and Le Roy have found disciples. In the valuable Bibliothèque Catholique des Sciences Religieuses a volume has just appeared on *Polytheism and Fetishism*, written by a Roman Catholic missionary in West Africa; it closes with a chapter on primitive revelation. The religion of primitive tribes in West Africa, the author says, always includes five elements, all of which are impossible to explain without accepting the fact that *God has spoken* (Heb. 1: 1). These five elements are: an organized family life; a name for a supreme, unseen Power, sovereign and benevolent; a moral sense, namely of truth, justice, shame, and a knowledge that there is good and evil; the idea of "soul" in every African language and the universal belief that this soul does not dies with the death of the body; and, finally, communion with the unseen supreme Power by prayer and sacrificial rites. "Devant ces considérations l'hypothèse de la Révélation primitive prend bien de la vraisemblance." [18] Before such considerations the hypothesis of a Primitive revelation takes on every appearance of truth.

The evolution hypothesis in religion has been overworked, and has seriously embarrassed students of religion who have grappled with the problem of sin, its

---

[17] *Religion of the Primitives.* Cf. Paul Radin, *Monotheism among Primitive Peoples,* London, 1924, pp. 65-67, and R. E. Dennett, *At the Back of the Black Man's Mind,* London, 1906, p. 168.

[18] R. P. M. Briault, *Polythéisme et Fétichisme,* Paris, 1929, pp. 191-195.

universality, and the universality of its correlate, namely *conscience,* that is a sense of sin as a subjective reality. In the history of religion, and in the study of the origin of the idea of God, we may no longer neglect the early chapters of Genesis and the statement of the Apostle Paul in the first chapter of his Epistle to the Romans.[19] Revelation, and not evolution, is the key to the origin of the idea of God and also, as we hope to show, of the origin of prayer and of sacrifice.

As Professor Paul Elmer More, in his little book, *The Sceptical Approach to Religion,* points out, in the study of non-Christian faiths

"sooner or later a more dispassionately comparative view of the whole subject is bound to reckon with the radically different as well as with the radically common features of religion. And the particular point it will have to consider is this: a monotheistic current, as we have seen, runs under the surface of all religions and apparently is at the source of the whole ethical experience and otherworldly belief of mankind, yet in one place only has this current worked itself out historically; why should this be?" [20]

[19] Cf. a special monograph by Emil Weber, *Die Beziehungen von Rom. 1-3 zur Missions praxis des Paulus,* Gütersloh, 1905.
[20] Princeton University Press, 1934, p. 156.

CHAPTER THREE
THE ORIGIN OF THE IDEA OF GOD

WHEREFORE God also gave them up to uncleanness through the lusts of their own hearts, to dishonour their own bodies between themselves: who changed the truth of God into a lie, and worshipped and served the creature more than the Creator, who is blessed for ever." Amen.

ROMANS 1:24, 25.

"Thereafter, as external civilization increased in splendor and wealth, so religion came to be expressed in forms of ever-increasing magnificence and opulence. Images of gods and daimones multiplied to an extent which defies all classification. Wealthy temples, shrines, and groves arose; more priests and servants, more sacrifices and ceremonies were instituted. But all this cannot blind us to the fact that despite the glory and wealth of the outward form, the inner kernel of religion often disappeared and its essential strength was weakened. The results of this, both moral and social, were anything but desirable, leading to extreme degradation and even to the deification of the immoral and antisocial. The principal cause of this corruption was that the figure of the Supreme Being was sinking further and further into the background, hidden behind the impenetrable phalanx of the thousand new gods and daimones."

W. SCHMIDT,
THE ORIGIN AND GROWTH OF RELIGION, *p. 289.*

CHAPTER THREE

THE ORIGIN OF THE IDEA OF GOD

SOME THIRTY-FIVE YEARS AGO ANDREW LANG, IN THE preface to his *Making of Religion,* spoke of his "anachronistic" views regarding the prevalence of a Skygod or Highest God among primitive tribes. His ideas, so bravely voiced in an age carried away by the evolutionary hypothesis, seemed absurd to most of his contemporaries and his great contribution to the study of the origin of religion was not appreciated (and was even ignored) until it was revived by Dr. W. Schmidt and others in our day, and so forced its way to recognition and wide acceptance by the new wealth of evidence gathered in corroboration, as we have already noted.

Through endless transformations, myths, and legends, the Sky-god or High-god is found at the base of all the ethnic religions in the Mediterranean area and in the Far East. We find him also among primitive tribes in most widely scattered areas and the belief in such a Supreme Spirit is characterized by a spontaneity,

76 THE ORIGIN OF THE IDEA OF GOD

universality, and persistency which can only point to a veritable primitive revelation or an innate perception.[1]

"Of the existence of a belief in a Supreme Being," wrote Andrew Lang, "among primitive tribes there is as good evidence as we possess for any fact in the ethnographic region." . . . "We shall show that certain low savages are as monotheistic as some Christians. They have a Supreme Being and the distinctive attributes of Deity are not by them assigned to other beings."[2]

How then did fetishism, magic, and ancestor-worship develop from such an early belief? Andrew Lang gives his answer; there was degeneration:

"Man being what he is, man was certain to 'go a whoring' after practically useful ghosts, ghost-gods, and fetishes which he could keep in his wallet or 'medicine bag.' For these he was sure, in the long run, first to neglect his idea of his Creator; next, perhaps, to reckon him as only one, if the highest of the venerable rabble of spirits or deities, and to sacrifice to him, as to them. And this is exactly what happened! If we are not to call it 'degeneration,' what are we to call it? It may be an old theory, but facts 'winna ding,' and are on the side of an old theory."[3]

All the startling facts on the side of this "old theory," all the mass of evidence from every part of the world, has now been collated and illuminated in the great work

---

[1] Kellogg, *Genesis and Growth of Religion*, pp. 172, 174. Cf. art. "Sky-gods" by Foucart in "Encyclopedia of Religion and Ethics." Also the remarks on the origin of religion by W. St. Clair Tisdall, *Comparative Religion*, pp. 1-15.

[2] *The Making of Religion*, pp. 181, 183.

[3] *Ibid.*, pp. 281, 282.

THE ORIGIN OF THE IDEA OF GOD

of W. Schmidt entitled *Der Ursprung der Gottesidee*. His five great volumes are an encyclopedia of facts, carefully documented, and represent every area of primitive culture.[4] His English work on *The Origin and Growth of Religion* is a mere summary in three hundred pages of the larger work numbering over 4,790 pages, and not yet completed.

We have already referred to this great work on Primitive Monotheism. It covers all those racial and tribal groups belonging to scattered stocks, not homogeneous, and thrust into remote places by later migrations.

"On the lower cultural levels are these: the Negritos of the Philippine Islands; various tribes of Micronesia and Polynesia; the Papuans of New Guinea; the black Aruntas of Australia; the Andaman Islanders in the Bay of Bengal; the Kols and Pariahs of Central and South India; the Pygmies and Bushmen of the Central African Congo basin; the Caribs of the West Indies; and the Yahgans of the extreme south of South America.

"On a higher plane are these: the Samoans and Hawaiians; the Kalmuks of Siberia; the Veddas of Ceylon; the Todas of the Nilgiri Hills, South India; the Bantu of south central and southern Africa; the Eskimos and the Amerinds [American Indians]."[5]

The geographical distribution of these groups when indicated by color on a world map show most graphic-

[4] Vol. i has 832 pp.; vol. ii, 1,063 pp.; vol. iii, 1,155 pp.; vol. iv, 820 pp.; and vol. v, 921 pp.

[5] This list is from J. K. Archer, *Faiths Men Live By*, pp. 18, 19, and follows in general Schmidt's classification.

78   THE ORIGIN OF THE IDEA OF GOD

ally that we deal with phenomena and facts of universal significance.

The last named group, the American Indians, are the special subject on which Dr. Schmidt gave a course of lectures in 1932 at Oxford,[6] and they occupy an entire volume in his larger work (vol. v). He demonstrates that "it is precisely among the three oldest primitive peoples of North America that we find a clear and firmly established belief in a High-god." Further,

"It is only now that we can produce the final proof that these High-gods, in their oldest form, come before all other elements, be they naturism, fetishism, ghost-worship, animism, totemism, or magism, from one or other of which the earlier evolutionistic theories had derived the origin of religion." (p. 19.)

Quite a large number of these tribes have not only a High-god, but have reached the idea that he is Creator *ex nihilo* of the visible universe.[7] And, speaking of the Algonquins, he summarizes eighty pages of evidence by saying:

"Thus we have in those religions a true God who is truly one; not a distant, cold 'originator,' but a true Supreme God, who is not afar off; not a stranger to men, but one who takes a keen interest in and exercises manifold influences on their life; whom also men do not consider as a stranger, but to whom they address themselves in a lively worship comprising a variety of prayers, sacrifices, and ceremonies."

[6] *High Gods in North America.*
[7] *Ibid.*, p. 131. *Ursprung der Gottesidee*, vol. v, pp. 473-554.

THE ORIGIN OF THE IDEA OF GOD

What is true of the Algonquins is equally true of other areas and races.

Grace H. Trumbull quotes from the ritual of the Omaha Indians, giving similar evidence, and it is from their own lips:

"At the beginning all things were in the mind of Wakonda. All creatures, including man, were spirits. They moved about in space between the earth and the stars. They were seeking a place where they could come into a bodily existence. . . .

"Dry land appeared; the grasses and the trees grew. The hosts of spirits descended and became flesh and blood. They fed on the seeds and grasses and the fruits of the trees, and the land vibrated with their expressions of joy and gratitude to Wakonda, the Maker of all things." [8]

The Supreme Being is generally represented in primitive tradition as absolutely good. He is called by various names denoting fatherhood, creative power, or residence in the sky. The name Father is used not by one tribe only, but among African Pygmies and Bushmen, by the Philippine Negritos, and in far-off Southeast Australia. The name Creator is not so widely distributed, but is common among the American Indians. The Ainu Supreme Being (in Northern Japan) has three beautiful names, viz.: Upholder, Cradle (of children), and Protector. [9]

The missionary Robert H. Nassau speaks of the idea of God among tribes where he has had forty years

[8] *Tongues of Fire*, p. 10.
[9] Schmidt, *Origin and Growth of Religion*, pp. 263-269.

80   THE ORIGIN OF THE IDEA OF GOD

residence, using their language and conversant with their customs:

"Under the slightly varying form of Anyambe, Anyambie, Njambi, Mzambi, Anzam, Nyam, or, in other parts, Ukuku, Suku, and so forth, they know of a Being superior to themselves of whom they themselves inform me that he is the *Maker* and *Father*. The divine and human relations of these two names at once give me ground on which to stand in beginning my address.

"If suddenly they should be asked the flat question, 'Do you know Anyambe?' they would probably tell any white visitor, trader, traveler, or even missionary, under a feeling of their general ignorance and the white man's superior knowledge, 'No! What do *we* know? You are white people and are spirits; you come from Njambi's town, and know all about him!' (This will help to explain what is probably true, that some natives have sometimes made the thoughtless admission that they 'know nothing about a God.') I reply, 'No, I am not a spirit; and, while I do indeed know about Anyambe, *I* did not call him by that name. It's your own word. Where did you get it?' 'Our forefathers told us that name. Njambi is the One-who-made-us. He is our Father.' Pursuing the conversation, they will interestedly and voluntarily say, 'He made these trees, that mountain, this river, these goats and chickens, and us people.'"[10]

And Father F. M. Savina, writing about the Miao race in China, says:

"The Miao hold an essentially monotheistic faith, they have never had a written language, they live in tribes and are an ancient people, having inhabited China before the present Chinese, and been pushed by them toward the

[10] *Fetichism in West Africa*, pp. 36, 37.

THE ORIGIN OF THE IDEA OF GOD

mountains in the south. . . . They believe in a Supreme Being, Creator of the world and of men. Death came as a consequence of man's sin; the woman had eaten white strawberries forbidden by the Lord of Heaven. They know of a deluge, followed by a dispersal of peoples. They believe in a life after death and in judgment: punishment and rewards and transmigration. They recognize good and evil spirits; the good are helpers, but God is directly petitioned to free men from the evil." [11]

The attributes of the High-god or Great Spirit, known by various names and in widely separated areas, are always nearly the same, namely: eternity, omniscience, beneficence, omnipotence, and power to give moral rewards and punishments. "A whole array of primitive peoples, the great majority, extend the Supreme Being's rewards and punishments to the other world. All primitive peoples without exception believe in another life." [12]

Another anthropologist, James W. Welch, states that the Northwestern corner of the Niger Delta is a virgin field for investigation and describes the Isoko people. He says:

"Their religion begins with the Supreme Being called Oghene, who is believed to have created the whole world and all peoples, including the Isokos. He lives in the sky which is a part of him, sends rain and sunshine, and shows his anger through thunder. *Oghene* is entirely beyond human comprehension, has never been seen, is sexless, and is only known by his actions, which have led men

[11] *Histoire des Miao*, Hongkong, 1930.
[12] Schmidt, *Origin and Growth of Religion*, pp. 270-275. Cf. vols. ii, iii, iv of *Ursprung der Gottesidee*.

to speak of *Oghene* as 'him,' because he is thought of as the creator and therefore father of all the Isokos. He is spoken of as Our Father, never as My Father. *Oghene* always punishes evil and rewards good." [13]

There is no missionary who has had a wider experience among Animistic heathen tribes than Johannes Warneck, superintendent of the Battak Mission in Sumatra. His book on *The Living Christ and Dying Heathenism* is a classic on the power of the Gospel and was epoch-making. He does not mince words in describing the horrors of heathenism, and yet he speaks of a root-idea in paganism

"very delicate and very difficult to discover, though deeply imbedded in the soul of the people. The eye, searching in the darkness, perceives the outline of a thought of some omnipotent power reigning over all those deities. Among the Battaks this is reflected in the general name, *Debata*, i.e., god. He is called simply god, also lord and grandfather. The idea which is here come upon of a supreme God is very vague, and is always in conflict with animistic feeling. All these chief gods and all great chiefs are called Debata. Great chiefs are to their subjects the highest beings, because they are most to be feared. Everything wonderful and worthy of veneration—ancestors, distinguished men, wild beasts, striking objects of a higher civilization—is called grandfather. The myths about the deities are not all the common possession of the people, but however dim the notions about them are, the heathen Battak divines in the *Debata*, the Lord who reigns over the universe in general and over man in particular. To him men turn instinctively in special distress. One often hears

[13] "The Isoko Tribe" in *Africa* (London), April, 1934.

THE ORIGIN OF THE IDEA OF GOD

in daily life expressions such as 'everything depends on God,' 'we are in God's hands,' 'that depends on God,' 'as God grants,' 'God is gracious.' There are beautiful proverbs about God—'A drop of dew with God's blessing makes a feast,' 'What God does man must not change,' 'God rises and looks down upon those who suffer wrong,' 'Do not follow crooked ways for riches come from God,' 'God is a righteous Judge,' 'Wherever we sit God is present.' "[14]

The most recent discussion of primitive monotheism is by Dr. Georg Wobbermin of the University of Göttingen in his lectures on *The Nature of Religion* (New York, 1933).

"The theory of primitive monotheism has had a long preliminary history. Although we must here entirely disregard the dogmatic theory of degeneration of the schoolmen, it must at least be mentioned that in certain rudimentary beginnings even David Hume, and then in the nineteenth century Creuzer, Schelling, and Max Müller, advocated a theory of primitive monotheism." (p. 356.)

He refers, also, of course, to the later works of Dr. Wilhelm Schmidt, who carried out Lang's idea and investigations more radically.

"For this purpose and also in order to prove his own theory which asserts a primitive monotheism in the strictest sense, Schmidt takes two paths. He attempts (1) to increase Lang's evidence; and (2) by means of critical study to formulate more convincingly that evidence. A discussion of this dual understanding of Schmidt from the point of view of the religio-psychological method should bring the whole problem nearer to a satisfactory solution."

---

[14] Joh. Warneck, *The Living Christ and Dying Heathenism*, p. 33.

But Wobbermin does not indicate in his appraisal of this evidence its accumulative and ubiquitous character. The detailed evidence regarding High-gods among all primitive tribes and accepted by ethnologists is given in summary by Schmidt, vol. i, pp. 632-700. He mentions the following: P. Ehrenreich, 1906; L. Von Schröder, 1914; J. H. Leuba, 1912; A. Titus, 1913; K. T. Preuss, 1914; K. Oesterreich, 1917; J. R. Swanton, 1917; A. L. Kroeker, 1907; A. Borens, 1918; Fr. Schleiter, 1919; Fr. Heiler, 1918; A. A. Goldenweiser, 1922; A. W. Niewenhuis, 1920; C. Brockelmann, 1922; R. Pettazoni, 1923; P. Radin, 1924.

All of these ethnologists deal chiefly with primitive religion and early cultural stages.

The evidence for primitive monotheism, however, is not limited to the legends, beliefs, and worship of primitive tribes. When we turn to the great ethnic religions of the past and of the present we meet with the same phenomena—a Sky-god or High-god who antedates polytheism, nature-worship, demonolatry, and ancestor-worship.

To begin with China and Japan:

"Dr. Timothy Richards, who lived for over half a century in China and knew the Chinese as well as any living European, writes: 'A Chinaman would consider it the greatest insult imaginable to speak of his countrymen as having no idea of the supreme God. Everyone I have ever met believes in the Supreme God far more than does the average man in Christendom!'" [15]

[15] Charles H. Robinson, *The Interpretation of the Character of Christ to Non-Christian Races*, p. 77.

THE ORIGIN OF THE IDEA OF GOD

Not to mention Legge and earlier scholars, Dr. John Ross of the United Free Church of Scotland wrote a book entitled *Primitive Monotheism in China*. In this volume he gathers evidence that seems indisputable:

"By neglecting the long past of China, when investigating the nature and probable sources of religion, philosophers and critics have missed an important element of information. Some modern theories would not have been so dogmatically ushered into the world, or so readily accepted when published, were the original religion of China familiar to the theorists. The 'ghost theory' of religion would scarcely have been broached, or the statement made that the spiritual form of religion known to us is the result of a long process of evolution from an original image-worship, had the story of the original religion of China been generally known.

"It is of some importance to note that the name given to God is similar in significance to the various names which we find in the Old Testament. The underlying concept of them all is 'power,' 'rule.' The Chinese name is composed of two separate words—*Shang*, meaning 'above,' 'superior to,' and *ti*, 'ruler'; the compound Shang-ti is Supreme Ruler, or 'King of kings, and Lord of lords.' The idea underlying the name Yahwe—the continually existing One—is implied in the uninterrupted use from unknown antiquity of the name Shangti.

"We fail to find a hint anywhere as to the manner how or the time when the idea of God originated in China, or by what process it came into common use. The name bursts suddenly upon us from the first page of history without a note of warning. At this point the very threshold of what the Chinese critics accept as the beginning of their authentic history, the name of God and other reli-

86 THE ORIGIN OF THE IDEA OF GOD

gious matters present themselves with the completeness of a Minerva." [16]

We have quoted at some length, for the facts relate to the largest mission field and the most populous. As regards Japan, we find a most interesting testimony by Professor Genchi Kato of the Imperial University at Tokio in a paper written for the Asiatic Society. He is dealing with the earliest form of Shinto:

"From what has been said above, it is natural and safest to say that Ama no Mi Naka Nusho no Mikoto is a manifestation of the so-called primitive monotheism.

"The thoughtful reader will perhaps be able to agree with my conclusion, that Ama no Mi Naka Nusho no Mikoto shows in its origin a clear trace of primitive monotheism when viewed in the light of the modern study of the science of religion." [17]

In ancient India we have Varuna, the most impressive deity among all the Vedic gods. He is the prehistoric Sky-god whose nature and attributes point to a very early monotheistic conception. He certainly dates from the Indo-Iranian period. "There is very much to be said in favour of regarding Varuna as originally the same as Ouranos," says Dr. Griswold. Varuna is the ethical god of the Hindu pantheon, merciful and gracious. Here are two stanzas from many prayers addressed to him in the Rigveda (vii: 89):

[16] *Primitive Monotheism in China*, pp. 18, 23, 25.

[17] "Transactions of the Asiatic Society of Japan," vol. xxxvi, pp. 159, 162. Cf. also *Le Shinto* by Genchi Kato. Paris: Paul Geuthner, 1931.

THE ORIGIN OF THE IDEA OF GOD

"I do not wish, King Varuna,
To go down to the home of clay,
Be gracious, mighty lord, and spare.

"Whatever wrong we men commit against the race
Of heavenly ones, O Varuna, whatever law
Of thine we here have broken through thoughtlessness,
For that transgression do not punish us, O god."

And these monotheistic ideas were not borrowed from Zoroastrianism. They were earlier.

"Scholars practically agree that Varuna equals Ahura Mazda, that is to say, the ethical god of the Rik is regarded as the same in origin as the ethical and supreme god of the Avesta. This means that a movement in the direction of ethical monotheism preceded the Indo-Iranian dispersion. This movement was not originated by the reformation connected with the name of Zoroaster, since that took place after the Indo-Iranian separation, probably as early as 1000 B.C." [18]

In the beautiful words of Max Müller, "There is a monotheism that precedes the polytheism of the Veda; and even in the invocations of the innumerable gods the remembrance of a God, one and infinite, breaks through the mist of idolatrous phraseology like the blue sky that is hidden by passing clouds." [19] The subject is so important that we give further testimony from a recent article in *Anthropos*:

"*Varuna* is omniscient. He knows everything, down to the secretest thoughts and desires of men. He numbers the winkings of every man's eyes; if a man were to flee

[18] Griswold, *The Religion of the Rig Veda*, pp. 24, 25.
[19] *History of Sanskrit Literature*, p. 559 (quoted in Kellogg, *Genesis and Growth of Religion*).

beyond the heavens he would still be seen by *Varuna* and his thousand *Spasas*. He is wise and universal lord. RV 1:25 says:

" 'Varuna, true to holy law (*Rta*) sits down among his people, he, most wise, sits there to govern all. From thence perceiving he beholds all wondrous things, both what hath been and what hereafter will be done. Thou, O wise God, are lord of all; thou art the king of earth and heaven.'

"Neither are these mere expressions of flattery to coax the god into granting favours. Max Müller had put forward a theory of Henotheism or Kathenotheism, but he had no followers. It is admitted by all modern scholars (Oldenberg, von Schroeder, Winternitz, Macdonell, Keith) that *Varuna* occupies a unique position in the early Rig-Veda. He is not just one of many gods, but the only God. this is why I have dwelt so long on *Varuna*. In the later Rig-Veda and in the Atharva Veda he sinks in importance, but still stands out among all the Vedic gods, *Indra* not excepted, as Professor Bloomfield remarks, 'like a god among men.'

"*Varuna* is already on the wane and yielding to the most boisterous and material Indra when the Rig-Veda opens. But even if we have no information of pre-Vedic times, we can judge from the progress in the Rig-Veda itself what the Vedic *Varuna* really was. He is never mentioned with an equal or rival. He is supreme God, till he disappears altogether and leaves his place to Indra. Though their attributes as monotheistic gods are not metaphysically explained and proved in the early Avesta and Rig-Veda, *Ahura Mazda* and *Varuna* are both lineal descendants of *Dyaus Pitar*, supreme creator and ruler of the universe and supreme judge of men's actions." [20]

[20] "Sin and Salvation in the Early Rig Vedas," by T. N. Siqueira of St. Xavier's College, India (in *Anthropos*, 1934).

THE ORIGIN OF THE IDEA OF GOD

The writings of ancient Egypt also witness to monotheistic belief in the midst of polytheism, and apparently of earlier date. "It is incontestably true," says Renouf, "that the sublimer portions of the Egyptian religion are not the comparatively late result of a process of development of elimination of the grosser. The sublimer portions are demonstrably ancient and the last stage of the Egyptian religion was by far the most corrupt." And he goes on to quote from another French scholar, Rougé: "The belief in the unity of the Supreme God and in his attributes as Creator and Lawgiver of man—these are primitive notions, encased like indestructible diamonds in the midst of the myths—logical superfetations accumulated in the centuries which have passed over the ancient civilization." [21]

We turn from Egypt to Assyria and learn that Ashur, the King-god, in the words of Olmstead, "was in many respects the precursor of Yahweh..... Each nation was at about the same period well on the road to monotheism. And then came the parting of the ways: Yahweh entered upon that unexampled development which led to the Christian Jehovah; Ashur succumbed

[21] Renouf, *Origin and Growth of Religion*, p. 95. "We will not go astray," says Alfred Blum-Ernst, "if we posit for the early Egyptians, next to their zoölatry and polytheism, a monotheistic tendency. It is not, however, the result of a development, but rather a heritage of primeval date." He then quotes at length from the Egyptologist Brugsch, who concludes: "Die zahllosen Fälle, in welchen mit aller Klarheit und Deutlichkeit des Verständnisses der Aegypter von Gott spricht oder sich an Gott wendet, erwecken den Glauben, als sei bereits in den frühesten Zeiten der ägyptischen Geschichte die eine, namenlose, unerfassliche, ewige Gott in seiner höchsten Reinheit von den Bewohnern des Niltales bekannt und verehrt worden."

to the miasma of Shumer. In the best Sumerian days, however, the worship of Ashur approached monotheism." [22]

In another passage and speaking of a longer hymn of praise carved on a statue of Nabu he says: "The author of this profession of faith has felt henotheism far behind and has almost reached pure monotheism with its intolerance of other gods, for he solemnly concludes: 'Trust not in any other god.'" [23]

When we come to consider the Arabs of ancient Arabia, long before the days of Mohammed, we find here also monotheistic belief preceding their later polytheism and nature-worship.

"The pagan Arabs, before Mohammed's time, knew their chief god by the name of *Allah* and even, in a sense, proclaimed his unity. In pre-Islamic literature, Christian or pagan, *ilah* is used for any god and *Al-ilah* (contracted to *Allah*), i.e., ὁ Θεος, *the* god, was the name of the Supreme. Among the pagan Arabs this term denoted the chief god of their pantheon, the Kaaba, with its three hundred and sixty idols. Herodotus informs us (Lib. II, cap. viii) that in his day the Arabs had two principal deities, *Orotal* and *Alilat*. The former is doubtless a corruption of *Allah Taal*, God most high, a term very common in the Moslem vocabulary; the latter is *Al Lat*, mentioned as a pagan goddess in the Koran. Two of the pagan poets of Arabia, Nabiga and Labid, use the word *Allah* repeatedly in the sense of a supreme deity. Nabiga says (Diwan, poem I, verses 23, 24): 'Allah has given them a kindness and grace

[22] A. T. Olmstead, *History of Assyria*, pp. 612, 653.
[23] *Ibid.*, p. 165.

which others have not. Their abode is *the* God (Al-ilah) himself and their religion is strong,' etc.

"Labid says: 'Neither those who divine by striking stones or watching birds, know what *Allah* has just created.'

"Al-Shahristani says of the pagan Arabs that some of them 'believed in a Creator and a creation, but denied Allah's prophets and worshiped false gods, concerning whom they believed that in the next world they would become mediators between themselves and Allah.' And Ibn Hisham, the earliest biographer of Mohammed whose work is extant, admits that the tribes of Kinanah and Koreish used the following words when performing the pre-Islamic ceremony of *ihlal:* 'We are present in thy service, O God. Thou hast no partner except the partner of thy dread. Thou ownest him and whatsoever he owneth.' " [24]

Professor D. C. Brockelmann of the University of Halle in a recent work deals with the question and rejects the view that Arabian monotheism was derived from Christian or Jewish sources.[25] He examines

"Wellhausen's view that Allah owes his existence to the peculiarities of the Arabic language, in which each tribe fell into the way of calling its own deity simply 'God,' with the result that the particular gods gradually disappeared. This view also Brockelmann rejects.

" 'It is impossible,' he says, 'to understand how this general name could have raised itself so decidedly over the specific ideas that it could triumphantly survive their annihilation'; and he rightly conjectures 'that Wellhausen, when he put forward this theory, was more or less con-

[24] Zwemer, *The Moslem Doctrine of God,* pp. 24-26.
[25] "Allah und die Götzen, der Ursprung der Vorislamischen Monotheismus," in Archiv für Religionswissenschaft, vol. xxi, pp. 99-121.

92 THE ORIGIN OF THE IDEA OF GOD

sciously under the influence of the hypotheses put forward by the British school of anthropology under E. B. Tylor, of whose supporters in the field of Semitic studies Robertson Smith and besides him Wellhausen have exercised the strongest directing influence on studies of the history of religion.' 'It is well known that the most important tenet of this school is the origin of the idea of God from animism. . . . . Thus, as Wellhausen, after the fashion of this school, supposed animism to be the only source of the religious life, logical consistency impelled him to derive the Arabian Allah, who could not be evolved directly from animism, out of animistic deities by the way of a process of abstraction.' "[26]

In view of all this it is preposterous to find the liberal school of Bible interpreters denying that Moses was a monotheist and making Yahweh a local thunder-god of the Sinai peninsula,[27] or tracing the religion of Israel from animism and totemism to the early prophets who were the first monotheists.[28]

On the contrary, the most ancient traditions of the race represent mankind as having commenced existence in a divine fellowship, and as having lost this estate only through sin. Such a view of the origin of religion has prevailed from the beginning of traceable history among all nations of the earth, varying only to such slight extent as would permit polytheistic peoples to conceive of the primeval divine fellowship polytheistically, and the monotheistic peoples monotheistically. To

[26] Schmidt, *Origin and Growth of Religion*, pp. 192, 193.
[27] Barton, *Semitic and Hamitic Origins*, pp. 325, 328, 334.
[28] W. O. E. Oesterley and T. H. Robinson, *Hebrew Religion: Its Origin and Development*, pp. 6-21, 194-201.

THE ORIGIN OF THE IDEA OF GOD

a monotheist it is significant that several of the ancient nations, representing widely different races, as for example the Egyptians, the Persians, the Chinese, seem to have been more monotheistic in their earliest conceptions of religion than in their later and latest creed and practice. But without dwelling upon this it may be stated as a broad and impressive fact that, with the exception of a few speculative authors, the solid traditional belief of the whole human family, in every age of the world, has been that man began his existence pure and sinless, and in conscious and intelligent divine communion. The golden age is put in the past. What is this than the biblical doctrine of the origin and first form of religion among men? What other theory can account for all the facts, even those relating to primitive races? The answer is not far to seek—and it comes from a scientist.

John R. Swanton, the President of the Anthropological Society of Washington, in an address on *Some Anthropological Misconceptions,* given on the occasion of his retirement from the presidency, spoke of the various evolutionary theories from Spencer to Frazer as follows:

"All of these theories are, it will be seen, particularistic. Each selects one particular feature from the mass of phenomena and arranges the rest in a series ending with the dominant belief of civilized man. As in the other cases, some element of belief particularly strange to so-called 'civilized' people is selected to start the series, and *each* chain of evolution leads dutifully up to either the monotheism or the atheism of western Europe.

"As in the other cases one answer to these theories is that the selection of one feature rather than another lacks validity, and that the arrangement of the evolutionary step is arbitrary. Furthermore, instead of being scattered through different peoples which might then be considered to represent so many distinct stages in the evolution of religion, one or more of these elements are frequently found in tribes equally primitive. . . . . In fact, the data at hand up to this point suggest that each element thus seized upon as a point of origination has in fact had an independent and parallel history. *Even in the case of our regnant monotheism it is a fair question whether it does not tie on to a belief in a sky-god extending back to the earliest days of religion among men, the only change which it has undergone being the relatively greater importance and deeper spiritualization of the concept in later times.*" [29]

Clement C. J. Webb, in his lectures on *Religion and Theism* delivered at Liverpool University in 1933, discussed the psychological accounts of the origin of belief in God, pointing out that "the explanation offered by psychologists of the nature of the idea of God do not answer the question about the origin of that idea put by such thinkers as Descartes, who found no satisfactory solution except in the assertion of the reality of such a Being as the idea in question represents to us." [30]

In the study of the origin and growth of religion the primary question is the idea of God. And this idea of

[29] *American Anthropologist*, vol. xix (1917), pp. 459-470.
[30] Clement C. J. Webb, *Religion and Theism*, p. 93.

a High-god, a Sky-god, a Supreme Spirit, we have seen, is too widespread to be ignored.

In conclusion, therefore, we ask how, apart from the Bible, are we to explain the origin of this almost universal tradition of the High-god among primitive tribes and in the ancient ethnic religions?

We undoubtedly have to recognize two factors, the one subjective, the other objective. The subjective factor we find in the nature of man as constituted by special creation. He bears the image of God. He is naturally endowed with a religious faculty. He is, even according to scientific nomenclature, *homo sapiens,* the type of anthropoid that is conscious of knowledge—in this case the knowledge of a Creator.

There is abundance of Scripture proof for this unique place of man in the universe and for these innate powers of his soul. And this scriptural evidence is corroborated by missionary experience in all lands. In other words, man is capable of knowing his Maker. The other factor is objective. The Creator is capable of making himself known to his creature. Dr. Kellogg expresses in a paragraph the need and the reasonableness of such an objective revelation:

"A man may have eyes, but as long as he is shut up in a dark cave he cannot see. So a man might have a faculty of apprehending God and his relation to him, but without a revelation of him he could not have a religion. The phenomena which are presented in the existence and the history of religion would still be inexplicable, except we assume, not merely a natural capacity in man for forming

96   THE ORIGIN OF THE IDEA OF GOD

religious conceptions, but also, correlated with these, a revelation of God to man, both original and universal. It is not indeed necessary, in order to account for the facts, to suppose that such a revelation must have been given it in a supernatural manner. Even Holy Scripture does not so represent the case. But an objective revelation, in some way, of the existence, and to some extent, of the character, of God, there must have been from the beginning, or the phenomena presented in religion are unaccountable." [81]

Some fifty years ago Dr. Francis L. Patton discussed the origin of Theism and, after giving the various theories of his day, came to conclusions which are now corroborated by the data collected in the great work of Dr. W. Schmidt and from the standpoint of anthropological science.

"If we may so express it, Adam derived his Monotheism by Inspiration, and we have derived ours from Revelation. This, however, is only a partial statement of the case.

"Setting aside the distinction between Revelation and Inspiration, it is easy to see that the question between those who advocate the theory of development on the one hand, and that of Revelation on the other, is whether man has attained to his idea of God by slow stages and his own unaided efforts, or whether he had it to begin with and by Divine communication. It is the question whether history has been an improvement or a degradation. It is one form of the great debate between the natural and the supernatural, in which so much that is precious is involved." . . . .

And in a later paragraph he goes on to say:

[81] Kellogg, *Genesis and Growth of Religion*, p. 171. Cf. Hodge, *Systematic Theology*, vol. i, pp. 191-303.

THE ORIGIN OF THE IDEA OF GOD

"There is a natural Theism as well as a revealed Theism; and this natural Theism is a factor in our Monotheism. The question is, whether this natural Theism is to be regarded as an inference or as an intuition. Those who hold that belief in one God is the slow growth of the centuries, hold that the theistic concept is an inference; but those who hold that belief in God is an inference do not necessarily hold that it was crude in its beginnings. The advocates of development theories generally assume that primitive man was incapable of reasoning in any other way than by supposing that physical objects are alive. But why should the causal judgment be developed only in this crude form? Why should primitive man be assumed to have no conscience? Why should the idea of the Infinite, or of necessary being, not present itself to his mind? And why is it unreasonable to suppose that before men became corrupt and degraded, as the result of sin, they were able to go by a direct inferential process, from their own existence to the existence of one God? It may be said that this view presupposes the fact of Revelation. No, it does not. It simply follows from the conclusions that have been reached regarding primitive Henotheism that if the theistic concept is an inference it started as a very pure and complete inference. Primitive Henotheism, in this respect, is in remarkable accord with the Bible's account of the beginnings of human history. . . . .

"We find, therefore, when we examine our belief in one living, personal God, that we cannot put our explanation of it under any one of the four categories that have been named. It is made up of different elements; and among them will be found the indwelling presence of God himself, the unconscious inference whereby we grasp the idea of dependence and a Being on whom we are dependent in one indivisible synthesis, the historic proof and elaborate defenses of a reasoned Theism, and the progressive revelations of the inspired Word." [32]

In this connection it is of interest to note that although Calvin's doctrine of the knowledge of God and of Common Grace was wholly based on the Scriptures, this very doctrine is now largely confirmed by anthropology and the history of religion. He held that in every man there is still a seed of religious truth and an ineradicable consciousness of God. Light is still shining in the darkness and all men still retain a degree of love for the truth, for justice and a social order. This knowledge of God, said Calvin, is innate but quickened by the manifestation of God in nature. It fails in its proper effect because of sin, and could only be restored by special grace in a special objective revelation.[33]

We conclude therefore that the origin of the idea of God is not due to magic, fetishism, manism, animism, or any process of evolution on man's part, but to God himself, the Creator of man and his Redeemer. "For ever since the world was created, his invisible nature, his everlasting power and divine being, have been quite perceptible in what he has made. So they have no excuse. Though they knew God, they have not glorified him as God nor given thanks to him; they have turned to futile speculations till their ignorant minds grew dark. . . . . Since they have exchanged the truth

[32] *The Presbyterian Review*, October, 1882, pp. 732-760.
[33] Benjamin B. Warfield, *Calvin's Doctrine of the Knowledge of God*, and Herman Bavinck, "Calvin and Common Grace," in *Calvin and the Reformation*, New York, 1909, pp. 118, 119, 133-137.

THE ORIGIN OF THE IDEA OF GOD

of God for an untruth, worshiping and serving the creature rather than the Creator who is blessed for ever. Amen." (Rom. 1: 20, 21, 25.)

The remaining chapters of this book are corroborative testimony, from many anthropological angles and a score of outstanding authorities, that the theory of evolution has many gaps and difficulties. The primitive myths as to the origin of man and of the world, the universality of prayer to an unseen Great Spirit, the idea of atoning blood-sacrifice, the universal association of the divine presence with fire, the sacredness of marriage and the universal belief in immortality—all of these do not confirm but combat the idea of religion as based on evolution.

CHAPTER FOUR

THE ORIGIN OF THE WORLD AND OF MAN

"WHERE wast thou when I laid the foundations of the earth? Declare if thou hast understanding. Who determined the measure thereof if thou knowest? Or who stretched the line upon it? . . . When the morning stars sang together and all the sons of God shouted for joy?"

JOB 38: 4-7.

"Then there was neither aught nor naught. No sky nor anything above it. What covered all, and where, by what protected? Was it water or deep darkness?

"Death was not there, nor immortality; nor confines of day and night. But that One breathed calmly alone; other than the One existed nothing which since hath been. Darkness was concealed in darkness in the beginning; indistinguishable water was all this universe.

"But the living force which lay enveloped in the husk at length burst forth from fervent heat. Through desire, the primal seed of mind, arose creation; desire known to the wise as the bond of being and non-being."

RIG-VEDA X: 129.

CHAPTER FOUR

THE ORIGIN OF THE WORLD AND OF MAN

"EVERY RELIGION AND EVERY MYTHOLOGY," SAYS James Freeman Clarke, "has held to the same formula: From Chaos to Cosmos."[1] All races of men in all times and from the earliest records have agreed in a most remarkable way in assuming a beginning of the universe and a process of creation by a Creator. Aristotle and Cicero are said to have expressed the opinion that "the universality of any conviction is a proof of its truth." As Hooker puts it: "The general and perpetual voice of men is as the sentence of God himself. For that which all men have at all times learned, Nature herself must needs have taught; and God being the author of nature, her voice is but his instrument."[2]

Before we discuss the universality of this evidence for creation and the origin of man, it may be well to recall the words of the Scripture in all their sublimity and lofty uniqueness as we compare them with the cosmogonies of the ethnic religions and the legends of primitive tribes. "In the beginning God created the

[1] *Ten Great Religions*, vol. ii, p. 196.
[2] *Ecclesiastical Polity*, book i, ch. viii: 3.

heavens and the earth. And the earth was without form and void and darkness was upon the face of the deep. And the Spirit of God moved upon the face of the waters. And God said, Let there be light, and there was light." Here theism comes to its own on the very first page of the Bible against every form of atheism, materialism, and pantheism. "The first of ancient books (Genesis) is the first of modern books; indeed, so to speak, it is the author of them all, for from its pages were to proceed all the languages, all the eloquence, all the poetry, and all the civilization that later times have known." [3]

The current theories regarding the origin of the universe may be reduced to four: (1) It had no origin and existed from eternity; (2) it came by a process of self-unfolding or evolution; (3) it came by a process of emanation; or (4) it was created by some higher intelligent Being. Although the second and fourth are not necessarily exclusive. The first of these theories has never been the belief of mankind anywhere. Chaos is first in every system of Cosmogony and cosmos is the result of a process or of a power that overcomes chaos. We read in the laws of Manu, "The universe existed in darkness, imperceptible, undefinable, as if immersed in sleep." Then came creation. The Phoenicians taught that "at the beginning of all things there was a dark condensed air, a turbid and black chaos." We find the same idea in the creation-myths of the Aztecs in Mexico and of the primitives in Polynesia.

[3] Ozanam, *La Civilisation au Vme Siécle*, vol. ii, p. 147.

ORIGIN OF WORLD AND OF MAN

According to Brinton (*Myths of the New World*), one can read in the picture-writing of the Aztecs this parallel to the first chapter of Genesis: "In the year and day of clouds, before years and days, the world lay in darkness; all things were without order; a water covered the slime and the ooze."[4]

The notion of evolution is found among many races, sometimes combined with an original creation. The origin of all things is traced to a world-egg or world-seed from which the universe is developed. From very early times some nations have been obsessed with the idea that *progenitiveness* was the key to unlock the mystery of existence. Sex-worship, together with the philosophy of a dual principle back of all life, is here found closely associated. The Shinto cosmogony of Japan is a striking example. Here there is no creation proper. Chaos contained germs like a world-egg and then we have personifications of the sky and earth, Izanagi-no-Mikoto and Izanami-no-Mikoto—the male and the female deities-who-invite—and give birth to the god-of-fire, etc.[5] Babylonia and Egypt have similar myths of Bel and Beltu or of *Nu* (the primeval deep) and *Nut*, the sky from which all things originated.[6] In ancient China we have something not unlike this dualism: "Before the beginning of all things there was Nothing. In the lapse of ages Nothing coalesced into Unity, the Great Monad. After more ages, the Great

[4] Clarke, *Ten Great Religions*, vol. ii, p. 195.
[5] W. G. Aston, *Shinto, The Way of the Gods*.
[6] W. St. Clair Tisdall, *Christianity and Other Faiths*, pp. 50, 51.

106 ORIGIN OF WORLD AND OF MAN

Monad separated into duality, the male and female principles of Nature: and then by a process of biogenesis the visible universe was produced." Popular cosmogony goes on to relate how a being called *P'an Ku* came into existence who constructed the world through his death. His breath became the wind; his voice, thunder; his left eye, the sun; his right eye, the moon; his hair, roots and plants; his flesh, the soil; his sweat descended as rain; while the parasites which infested his body were the origin of the human race![7] Here there is no mention of Shangti, the Supreme Ruler, as Creator.

The curious reader will find a full account of the cosmogonies of the various ethnic faiths in the Encyclopedia of Religion and Ethics. Most of these are based on development or emanation theories, although a few bear some resemblance to the creation story of Genesis.

We are more concerned with the beliefs of primitive religion as found in the legends and myths of aboriginal tribes. These generally believe in a Creator or High-god who is cause of the visible creation, and without whom nothing came into existence. Wilhelm Schmidt has collected all of these creation stories in detail and with documentary evidence, from many observers.[8] In volume ii, for example, we find the creation-myths of the following Indian tribes: Arapaho (pp. 684-717), Cheyenne (pp. 759-763), Gros Ventres (pp. 673-676), Menominee (pp. 550-561), Pomo (pp.

[7] Giles, *Religions of Ancient China*, pp. 7, 8.
[8] *Ursprung der Gottesidee*, vol. ii, with pages as indicated.

211-214), Yuki (pp. 58-62), and especially the Winnebago (pp. 618-635). All these creation stories have great similarity and yet their variety is positive proof that they are indigenous and not due, as some have supposed, to the infiltration of ideas from missionary contacts.

As a specimen from another source than Schmidt, we give the creation-story of the Indians of Guatemala, translated by Bancroft from their own language, Quiché:

"The heaven was formed, and its boundaries fixed toward the four winds by the Creator and Former—the Mother and Father of all living things—he by whom all move, the father and cherisher of the peace of men, whose wisdom has planned all things.

"There was as yet no man, nor any animal, nor bird, nor fish, nor green herb, nor any tree. The face of the earth was not yet seen, only the peaceful sea and the space of heaven. Nothing was joined together, nothing clung to anything else, nothing balanced itself, there was no sound. Nothing existed but the sea, calm and alone, immobility and silence, darkness and night.

"Alone was the Creator, the Former, and the feathered serpent, enveloped in green and blue, their name Gu-cu-matz, or Feathered Serpent. They are the heart of heaven. They spake together and consulted, mingling their thoughts. They said 'Earth,' and earth came, like a cloud or fog. Then the mountains arose, and the trees appeared, and Gu-cu-matz was filled with joy, saying 'Blessed be thy coming, O Heart of Heaven! our work is done!'" [9]

[9] Clarke, *Ten Great Religions*, vol. ii, pp. 200, 201.

We also find similar creation myths in the Andaman Islands;[10] among the Semang pygmies of Malay;[11] the Samoyeds of the Arctic, whose High-god, Num, is creator of all things;[12] the Ainu of Japan;[13] the Kulin of Australia;[14] and the Pygmies of West Equatorial Africa.[15] Other creation stories are given by Schmidt as found among the Batwa of Ruanda in Africa and elsewhere. The Ituri-Pygmies of Central Africa, he says, are an exception to the rule, as they have no creation myths.

We have already referred in Chapter III to the beautiful account of creation given in the Omaha Indian ritual. Here is a fragment from the Maori poem of creation as given by J. C. Andersen: "The night had conceived the seed of night. The heart, the foundation of night, had stood forth, self-existing even in gloom. It groweth in gloom, the life pulsating and the cup of life. The shadows screen the faintest ray of light. . . . . The procreative power, the ecstasy of life first known. . . . . Thus the progeny of the Great-extending filled heaven's expanse. The chorus of life arose and swelled into ecstasy, then rested in bliss of calm and quiet." [16]

What a distant echo this is of the creation as described in the book of Job, when God laid the founda-

[10] Schmidt, *Ursprung der Gottesidee*, vol. iii, pp. 65-68.
[11] *Ibid.*, p. 230.
[12] *Ibid.*, pp. 352 ff.
[13] *Ibid.*, pp. 446, 447.
[14] *Ibid.*, pp. 674-682.
[15] *Ibid.*, vol. iv, pp. 26-39.
[16] Turnbull, *Tongues of Fire*, p. 11.

tions of the earth while "all the morning stars sang together and the sons of God shouted for joy."

And from the far-off island Tahiti we have a similar hymn of creation:

"He abideth, Taaroa by name, in the immensity of space. There was no earth, there was no heaven, there was no sea, there was no mankind.

"Taaroa calleth on high; he changed himself fully. Taaroa is the root, the rocks, the sands; Taaroa stretcheth out the branches; Taaroa is the light; Taaroa is within; Taaroa is below; Taaroa is enduring; Taaroa is wise. He created the land of Hawaii, Hawaii great and sacred, as a cruse for Taaroa." [17]

When we study the attributes of the primitive Highgod as held in the various culture areas already mentioned from the Arctic to Tierra del Fuego, we find everywhere not only a sort of eternity ascribed to him, but omniscience, beneficence, morality, and above all omnipotent creative power. "The Supreme Being," says Schmidt, "is recognized as Creator more or less definitely among all Pygmy peoples, concerning whom we have anything like full information; also among the Ainu, the Southeast Australians, the oldest Tierra del Fuego people, and most especially among the primitives of the American Northwest and North Central Californians, the Algonquin and the Winnebago. In this last group we find the idea of Creation in its highest form, that of creation *ex nihilo* expressed with the

[17] Turnbull, *op. cit.*, p. 12. Both quoted from Paul Radin, *Primitive Man as Philosopher*.

greatest definiteness and explicitness."[18] The Winnebago Indians have great tribal ceremonies which are representations and repetitions of their creation story.

The creation of man is often the subject of special legends, some of which have points of resemblance to the Scriptures. In North Central California, according to Schmidt, three methods are described.

"In the first, man was made from birds' feathers; this probably is due to totemic influences. In the second, he was made from sticks, which became human overnight. In the third, his body was formed out of clay, and life was put into the bodies of clay overnight by the Supreme Being sweating amongst them. Amongst the Kulin of Southeast Australia, the body is made of clay and the Supreme Being breathes life into it through the nose, mouth, and navel. Among the East Kenta Semang also, Kari makes two children out of clay for his wife Manoid; among the Kensiu Semang he makes them out of fruits, but nothing is said of a separate creation or immission of the soul. Among the Gabon Pygmies the Supreme Being makes the body of the first man of wet clay, and gives it life by his almighty word. Among the Ainu, God makes the skeleton out of a piece of wood and fills in the gaps with earth."[19]

It is worthy of remark that in most of these primitive accounts of creation, the creation of man is told in a special form. He is the culmination of creation. The High-god completed his work when he made man. The same is true in some of the ethnic religions.

According to Zoroaster, "the first creation of Ahura

[18] Schmidt, *Origin and Growth of Religion*, p. 272.
[19] *Ibid.*, p. 273.

Mazda was the sky; the second, water; the third, soil; the fourth, plants; the fifth, animals; the sixth, mankind." This very closely follows the order in Genesis. Afterward God created a Paradise and introduced Mashya and Mashyoi, brother and sister, the ancestors of the race.

"God (Ahura Mazda) spake to Mashya and Mashyoi, saying, 'You are man, you are the ancestry of the world, and you are created perfect in devotion by me. Perform devotedly the duty of the law, think good thoughts, speak good words, do good deeds, and worship no demons.'

"And, afterward, antagonism rushed into their minds, and their minds were thoroughly corrupted, and they exclaimed that the Evil Spirit created the water and the earth, the plants and the animals and the other things named above. That false speech was spoken through the will of the demons, and the Evil Spirit possessed himself of his first enjoyment from them. Through that false speech they became wicked and their souls are in hell until the future existence." [20]

Then follows a long account of their banishment, of how they discovered the use of fire, made clothing of skins, and forged iron for tools. Somewhat later the Zoroastrian scriptures chronicle the story of the flood and the ark.[21]

The fact is that we often find side by side in these creation stories references also to the fall of man and to a great flood. Here again we have parallels to Genesis which are difficult to explain or to explain away.

[20] M. M. Dawson, *The Ethical Religion of Zoroaster*, p. 53.
[21] *Ibid.*, pp. 54-58.

The old idea that the primitive traditions of creation were crude, low, and childish needs modification, for "we may as well judge the wine by the dregs as to judge primitive man by the savage of today." Side by side with the most absurd myths we have the conception of a good Being who is the creator of all things and the guardian of the moral life of men.[22]

It is true that the demiurge at whose hand the great Spirit creates the world is often pictured as a boar, a fish, a hawk, a tortoise, or a coyote. In some cases these are symbols of wisdom or power, and again they may be identical with the totem of the tribe. In spite of immense diversities, therefore, we see a family likeness in the creation myths of the world even as we do in the case of the flood-myths, and this is very significant.[23] This flood-tradition of the human race also seems to testify to the historicity of the earlier chapters of Genesis. Frazer in his *Folk-lore in the Old Testament* gives a full list of these flood-stories. Other and earlier writers, however, do not consider them myths, but rather traditions of a common human experience. The subject has been carefully studied by a number of writers. Among the best known of these we may mention the Germans, R. Andree, H. Usener, E. Böklen, G. Gerland, and, at a much earlier date, Philipp Buttman. Besides these there were the Aus-

[22] Lang, *Myth, Ritual, and Religion*, i: 329.
[23] A. W. Nieuwenhuis, "Die Sintflutsagen als Kausal-logische Natur-Schöpfungsmythen," in *Festschrift* of P. W. *Schmidt*, Vienna, 1928, pp. 515-526. He collates hundreds of Flood-stories from every area of culture and compares them with similar creation-myths and legends.

train, M. Winternitz, and the French savant, Francois Lenormant. In a recent book on the evidence for a universal flood, Harold Peake says:

"One thing appears clear, namely, that none of these [flood-stories] bear any but quite accidental resemblance to the Hebrew story, except that recorded in Mesopotamia. These two stand apart from the others in many significant details, and, as we shall see in subsequent chapters, both relate to the same event, which can now be shown to have a strictly historical basis."

His interesting volume deals with the archaeological evidence for the truth of the flood-epic as related in the book of Genesis.[24]

We turn back, however, to the *creation* myths and traditions.

The religious history of Egypt, says J. Strachan, is "the history of a theism almost choked by an animism which defied beasts, birds, and trees."[25] Yet we find Ptah or Thoth represented as the master artisans, the Creators of the world. In a papyrus kept at Turin we read the following words put into the mouth of a Creator:

"I am the maker of heaven and of the earth, I raise its mountains and the creatures which are upon it: I make the waters..... I am the maker of heaven, and of the mysteries of the twofold horizon. It is I who have given to all the gods the soul which is within them. When I open my

[24] Harold Peake, *The Flood: New Light on an Old Story*, New York, 1930, pp. 14, 27, 95-116.
[25] "Encyclopedia of Religion and Ethics," vol. iv, p. 227.

eyes, there is light; when I close them, there is darkness."[26]

In the Indian cosmogony Varuna is called the creator of the universe, although the religion of the Vedas is polytheistic. And although fanciful and obscene myths are not few, we also have the sublime creation hymn quoted at the beginning of this chapter.

It is well known that the creation-epic of Babylonia has such resemblance to the Mosaic account that certain scholars claim it was the earlier. Professor A. H. Sayce, however, says that this epic of Marduk and Tiamat is of far later date than the Sumerian creation myths on which it is based.[27]

And Professor More, in comparing the creation myths with the early chapters of Genesis, says:

"As the story appears in Genesis (a relatively late version, re-written by some priestly scribe), the fantastic elements have been eliminated, or reduced to a minimum, while all the emphasis is laid on the creative power of Jehovah. The whole legend is simple and sublime, and even shows curious adaptability to a scientific theory of evolution. In passing from it to the Babylonian tablets it is as if one slipped from the sobriety of daylight into a succession of telescoping nightmares."[28]

The Greek cosmogonies may be divided into three classes: those that begin with a spiritual principle as Zeus; those beginning with an abstract principle as Chaos, Time, or Night; and those beginning with a

---
[26] "Encyclopedia of Religion and Ethics," vol. iv, p. 228.
[27] *Ibid.*, art. Cosmogony.
[28] *The Sceptical Approach to Religion* (1934), p. 148.

material principle, such as water, earth, and ether. Why should we say that the latter is the most primitive? It is *not* clear, as some writers tell us, that "the spiritual creation story by Zeus and its unitarian tendency is a later development." Why should not the early Greeks as well as the primitives of Africa and America have had the conception of a High-god who was the creator of the world and benefactor of man—the Zeus-pater, Jupiter, Heavenly Father?

Lewis Spence in his article on the cosmogony of the North American Indians calls attention to the similarity of their myth to the account in Genesis. The tribe he mentions lived east of the Mississippi and belonged to the Seminole family.

"The Muskhogees believe that before the Creation a great body of water alone was visible. Over the dreary waste two pigeons flew to and fro, and at last espied a blade of grass rising above the surface. Dry land gradually followed, and the mainland and the islands took their present shapes. In the center of the hill *Nunne Chaha* was the house of *Esaugetuh Emissee, the* 'Master of breath,' who molded the first man from the clay which surrounded his abode. The waters still covered the earth, so that he was compelled to build a great wall to dry the mud-fashioned men upon. When the soft mud had hardened into flesh and bone, he directed the waters to their present places, and gave the dry land to the men whom he had made. Here we cannot doubt that the appearance of the two pigeons signifies the brooding of the creative spirit upon the waste of waters." [29]

[29] "Encyclopedia of Religion and Ethics," vol. iv, p. 127.

Not only, as we have seen above in the legends and myths of the creation in general, but also in those relating to the creation of man are there strange coincidences and parallels to the record in Genesis. It is not easy to explain why the creation of man should be regarded as a special and extraordinary work of the High-god among primitives unless man occupies a place that is unique above all other creatures. Here no totemistic explanation can bridge the chasm. The whole animate and inanimate world is on one side, man is on the other. He belongs to a separate class. His moral nature and his immortal nature place him above the brutes. "On this point," as Clarke says, "the Hottentot and the Fiji Islanders agree with Plato and Aristotle." [30] "Our blacks," writes Le Roy, "have a morality whose basis is fundamentally just the same as that acknowledged by the conscience of the whole human species, whatever race, country, or period of development." [31]

At the back of the Black man's mind, therefore, and in his legends of creation, we have a consciousness of a special relation of the immortal human spirit to the Creator. Man is distinct from the cosmos. Among the Gabun Pygmies there are three creation-myths regarding man: He was made of clay and life injected when the Great Spirit said, "Get up!" Another story is that life came to the molded form of man (as in Michelangelo's "Creation of Adam"!) by the touch of

[30] *Ten Great Religions,* vol. ii, p. 163.
[31] Le Roy, *The Religion of the Primitives,* p. 168.

ORIGIN OF WORLD AND OF MAN

God's finger. In a third account man and his mate were made by God from the cola-nut.[82]

Among the Andamanese they say, "The High-god created the first man and his wife." The Semang Pygmies have other stories of a special creation. Schmidt sums up the evidence by saying: "The belief in man's special creation is well-nigh universal among all the Pygmy-tribes of Asia and Africa. They only differ regarding the manner of this creation."[83] Namely, to use his own words:

"Dit Mittel, durch welche der aus Lehm geformte oder in Früchten präexistente Leib des Menchen sein Leben erhält und dadurch zu einem wirklichen Menschenleib wird, sind: 1. Einfaches Liegenlassen die Nacht hindurch (Kenta); 2. Anstossen mit dem Finger; 3. Anhauchen; 4. Anspeien; 5. In-den-Mund-nehmen (die Formen 2, 3, 4, 5 bei den Gabun-Pygmäen)."

Nowhere is the creation of man placed on the level of the general creation of animals. A delightful story is told among the Gabun Pygmies in this connection: "When the first human pair were created the monkeys came from every side to look at them and to greet them, saying, 'We are your friends.' Then the Creator rebuked them and sent them back to their shelter saying, 'Man is not your friend, he is your lord.' "[84] That man is the lord of creation according to primitive religion is evident from the folk-lore of primitives, their taboos,

[82] Schmidt, *Ursprung der Gottesidee*, vol. vi, p. 499.
[83] *Ibid.*, vol. iv, pp. 758-761.
[84] *Ibid.*, vol. iv, p. 462.

their "faith, hope, and charity," and most of all, as we shall see later, in their defiance of death and belief in immortality.

Nevertheless, man is also conscious that he has lost his first estate. He questions the why and how of evil and death. These questionings we find give rise to innumerable myths which suggest as answer that in the distant past something had occurred which reduced man to his present state. Some great disaster has affected his destiny and robbed him of a former happier Golden Age. Some of these myths explain the presence of death and other evils by man's own fault in breaking a taboo. Or they tell how man lost his intercourse with God by sexual craving or by the instigation of a woman. The Dog-rib Indians say man lost an arrow which the Creator gave him to keep with great care, and then the High-god left the world and death entered. The Blackfoot Indians say the folly of a woman caused death to enter the world. The Polynesians tell of a Golden Age when death, war, and famine were unknown. Then, through a quarrel, death, disease, and famine came to mankind. More usually death is directly attributed to man's disobedience, eating of forbidden fruit or entering a forbidden area. "Some myths of this class," says J. A. MacCulloch, "bear a striking resemblance to the story in Genesis." He gives scores of examples from every part of the world, "many of which are undoubtedly original, even if a few might at first seem to be borrowed." For example:

"The Andamanese, whose remarkable theology, according to the best authorities, is independent of Christian influence, believe that Puluga, the creator, gave the first man, Tomo, various injunctions, especially concerning certain trees which grew only at one place (Paradise) in the jungle, and which he was not to touch at certain seasons—during the rains, when Puluga himself visits them and partakes. Later, some of Tomo's descendants disobeyed and were severely punished. Others, disregarding Puluga's commands about murder, adultery, theft, etc., and becoming more and more wicked, were drowned in a deluge. Two men and two women survived, and in revenge wished to kill Puluga, who, telling them that their friends had been justly punished, disappeared from the earth." [35]

So vivid is the memory of the effects of this fall and disobedience of man that the picture of a Golden Age in the past is common to all the great ethnic religions. In the words of Walter Lippman (who is surely an unprejudiced witness in such a matter):

"The memory of an age of innocence has haunted the whole of mankind. It has been a light behind their present experience which cast shadows upon it, and made it seem insubstantial and not inevitable. Before this life, there had been another which was happier. And so they reasoned that what once was possible must somehow be possible again. Having once known the good, it was unbelievable that evil should be final." [36]

The evidence of anthropology therefore seems to be that of an almost universal tradition of a creation of

[35] "Encyclopedia of Religion and Ethics," article Fall, vol. v, p. 707.
[36] *A Preface to Morals*, p. 151.

the world by a High-god in which man occupies a special place as its culmination. Moreover, we find together with this account of man's place in the universe and parallel to it a widely-spread tradition of man's displacement, of a tragedy of disobedience and the loss of his former state of happiness. Who can resist the conclusion that these many and multiform creation-myths, these constant memories of a lost "age of innocence" point to a common human tradition and corroborate the scriptural data?

Even from the standpoint of evolution the last word regarding the appearance of *Homo sapiens* has not been spoken. In the most recent book available, a popular treatise on the origin of man, we can see how far back his ancestry goes.

"Among the things which change very slowly in terms of human time (as distinct from geological and astronomical time)," says L. S. B. Leaky, "we may reckon physical evolution, and also belief in a life after death. We have seen that Stone Age man, especially toward the close of the Pleistocene period, buried his dead with elaborate care, and placed with them offerings of food and tools. From this we can only imply one thing. These Stone Age ancestors of ours—and also our Stone Age cousins the men of the Neanderthal species—believed in a life after death, and acted upon that belief, just as men do today, all over the world." [87]

[87] *Adam's Ancestors.* An Up-to-Date Outline of What Is Known about the Origin of Man. By L. S. B. Leaky. London: 1934. Methuen & Co., Ltd. Pp. 226-228.

And the scientist goes on to say a little later:

"Perhaps some readers of this book, when they realize that prehistory has now traced back man of our own type to the beginning of Pleistocene, and has shown that he was contemporary with various other more primitive types of man and not evolved from them, will begin to think that here is evidence which is contrary to the theory of evolution. It has been suggested to me that since the results of our work show that *Homo sapiens* has changed so little in the long period of time known as the Pleistocene, this may be taken to indicate that this type of man has his origin in a special creative act, and is not the result of any normal evolutionary process.

"This is certainly not the interpretation which I would put upon the available evidence. I should say rather that we have learned that *evolution has been very much slower* than we have sometimes been led to believe. The presence of four completely different types of man at the beginning of the Pleistocene suggests to me that their common ancestor must be looked for in deposits at least as old as the Miocene period. The further fact that in deposits of Miocene Age we have evidence of the existence of anthropoid apes very akin to those still living today must suggest that the common ancestor of man and the anthropoids will have to be sought in deposits of still greater age. There can be little doubt now that man has been in existence upon the earth much longer than the million years assigned to the Pleistocene period." [38]

Hence the imaginary link that binds man to the brute on the tree-of-ancestors is put back in time so far that the question of his origin becomes purely academic. *In*

[38] Leaky, *op. cit.*

the Miocene age anthropoids and men were already distinct species!

How much more reasonable is the fact of a special creation. Once we admit that the High-gods were earlier than animism and nature-worship, than magic and manism, there is an *a priori* argument for creation. For, as Coleridge says in his *Aids to Reflection,* "the moment we assume an origin in nature, a true beginning, an actual first, that moment we rise above nature and are compelled to assume a supernatural power." Compelled by what? By the demand for an adequate cause, a sufficient reason for the visible and tangible world that surrounds us. Primitive man, according to the creation-myths and legends, made this very deduction. "For the invisible things of Him from the creation of the world are clearly seen, being understood by the things that are made, even his eternal power and Godhead."

"In the beginning God created the heavens and the earth." "This statement," said Ernest Renan, "is like the cold mistral which cleared the sky, like the sweep of the broom which related far beyond our horizon the chimeras which darkened it. A free will, as amplied in the words, 'He created,' substituted for ten thousand capricious fancies is a progress of its kind. The great truth of the unity of the world and of the absolute solidarity of its parts which polytheism failed to appreciate, is at least clearly perceived in these narratives in which all parts of nature bring forth by the action of the same thought and the effect of the same verb. . . . .

What reads as grotesque in Berosus appears in the Bible narrative so true and so natural that we, with our western credulity, have treated it as history, and have imagined when we adopted these fables that we have been discarding mythology." [89]

It is, however, *not* mythology. No nomad shepherd could have invented this creation story. It is altogether different from the other cosmogonies. It bears the stamp of truth, by the objective evidence of anthropology in its contrasting stories of creation and myths often grotesque and absurd.

And the genesis of the world and of man as recorded on the first pages of the Bible leaves the impression of a sublimity and truthfulness and conviction that preclude all invention. Here we have not myth but fact. It is one total conception, perfect and consistent in all its parts, unequaled by any other creation-epic. "Genesis," as Luther says, "is a lofty book; we can never exhaust its meaning." And this is especially true when we use it as a source-book in the study of the history of religion. Here speaks a Voice; all else is echo.

[89] *The People of Israel*, vol. i, pp. 67, 68.

CHAPTER FIVE

THE ORIGIN OF PRAYER AND SACRIFICE

"Prayer—the Churche's banquet, Angel's age,
God's breath in man returning to his birth,
The soul in paraphrase, heart in pilgrimage,
The Christian plummet sounding heav'n and earth;

Engine against the' Almightie, sinner's towre,
Reversèd thunder, Christ-side-piercing spear,
The six-daies-world transposing in an houre,
A kind of tune which all things heare and fear;

Softnesse, and peace, and joy, and love, and bliss,
Exalted manna, gladnesse of the best,
Heaven in ordinarie, man well drest,
The milkie way, the bird of Paradise,

Church-bells beyond the starres heard, the soul's bloud,
The land of spices, something understood."

GEORGE HERBERT

"To express his relation to the supernatural world that dominates him, we shall find in the primitive's religion all the feelings that vivify the most elevated religions: submission, veneration, adoration, expressed by the lowered and prostrate position of the body; grief (which assumes special marks in case of mourning—white paint covering the whole body or merely the forehead, torn clothes, fasting, etc.); joy (indicated by certain ornaments of the body and of the costume, by dances and songs); purity or purification (obtained or symbolized by various means among which we must point out the use of lustral water); the desire of imitation, which creates an additional affinity between man and the object of his worship; that sort of aspiration in man for a visible and tangible God, which results in fetishism and idolatry."

LE ROY,
THE RELIGION OF THE PRIMITIVES, *p. 195.*

CHAPTER FIVE
THE ORIGIN OF PRAYER AND SACRIFICE

PRAYER IS UNDOUBTEDLY THE OLDEST AND MOST UNIversal of all religious rites. It is perhaps even older than sacrifice, for it lies at the root of the latter. There are certain tribes in Australia where prayer exists, but where the rite of sacrifice is unknown[1] and originally the rite of sacrifice was the greeting and acknowledgment of obeisance to the one to whom the worshiper presented a petition or gave thanks.

Yet the two are closely related in all primitive religion as they are in the great ethnic religions of the past and in the living religions of our day.

Professor Archer, in speaking of sacrifice and prayer, says that "two constant elements among all the higher primitives who recognize nature-powers as gods are offering and prayer."

"Sometimes the offering is of blood in expiation, to cleanse the people of their sins. When the flesh of the slaughtered animal is consumed in part by priest and people, it strengthens the whole tribe; and when portions of the offering are burnt, the odor rising on high is pleasing

[1] Heiler, *Das Gebet*, p. 72.

128   ORIGIN OF PRAYER AND SACRIFICE

to the nostrils of the gods. Sacrifice is not a simple, but a complex rite, even among primitive peoples.

"Offerings are accompanied by prayers; man voices his intent before the gods, telling his simple needs. Now prayer, and possibly sacrifice, is, strictly speaking, on a higher than magical level, for prayer is a recognition of superhuman powers which must be petitioned, not coerced. Primitive prayers are, however, scarcely more than declarations, praise, and petitions. They are for the most part extempore, but since the occasions of prayer are more or less constant, the prayers often assume apparently fixed forms." [2]

Whatever the form of prayer among primitive races, the fact of prayer is universal. There is no tribe or people, however degraded or ignorant of even the beginnings of civilization, that does not pray. In all ages and in all lands men have called upon their gods, invisible spirits, or the Great Spirit, and poured out their needs.

The motive of this universal practice must be either an urge to prayer from within or from without. Men began to pray and continued to pray, either because their petitions were answered and they received blessing, or they began and continued to pray because the necessity of their moral nature bade them commune with the Unseen. As Augustine said, "O God, thou hast made us for thyself and our hearts find no rest until they rest in thee."

"In the earliest existing documents," says Grace H. Turnbull, "there already comes to light the ceaseless

[2] John Clark Archer, *Faiths Men Live By*, p. 41.

ORIGIN OF PRAYER AND SACRIFICE

searching after God if haply he might be found; and the unanimity of this quest all down the ages is the surest evidence of man's need of Deity. Whatever this straining after God might signify, whether he can be expressed in human terms or not, whether he is but the projection of our own highest ideals, no study is more uplifting than the attempt through the centuries of man's eager, often crude attempt to overtake his Creator and portray him in all his blinding glory to our mortal eyes.

"As far into the remote reaches of existence as we can penetrate, we find too the persistent ideas of holiness and righteous living, however that ideal may very from age to age. Strange, how this notion of holiness (*wholeness*) first entered human thought! Yet there it is, voicing itself in admonitions and aspirations very like our own, in prayers that might have been written yesterday, in lives that approach the Christian ideal if not that of Christ himself!"[3]

Not only is the fact of prayer universal among primitive races, but more and more the evidence is accumulating that the most primitive prayers were addressed to a Supreme Being. And a study of prayers among primitive peoples contributes its testimony that monotheistic ideas preceded the worship of many gods and that the earliest form of religion in China and India, not to mention ancient Egypt, was monotheistic.

Thus among the backward races such as the American Indians or the Bushmen of South Africa we find prayer addressed to a Great Spirit. In the South Sea Islands and among some of the hill tribes of India, the Great Spirit is even called Father-of-All.

[3] Grace H. Turnbull, *Tongues of Fire*, p. xxiii.

The study of non-Christian religions reveals the fact that God has not left himself without a witness among all nations and that his common grace is shed abroad in human hearts even where no knowledge of the Gospel has illuminated the soul. For it is true of the non-Christian world as of our own that

> "Prayer is the soul's sincere desire,
>   Uttered or unexpressed;
> The motion of a hidden fire
>   That trembles in the breast.
> Prayer is the burden of a sigh,
>   The falling of a tear,
> The upward glancing of an eye
>   When none but God is near." [4]

Prayer is the ladder between earth and heaven. The man who prays belongs to two worlds; the prayerless man to only one. The man who prays looks up to powers higher than himself and so is made better. We gladly recognize that even among primitive savages prayer is a means of strengthening emotion, sustaining courage, and awakening hope.

Prayer among the ancient Greeks was woven into their public and private life. As a rule they prayed in short formulas which they believed had a magical power. Plato says, "Every man of sense before beginning any important work will ask help of the gods." Plutarch tells of the great orator Pericles that before he began an address he always prayed the gods to make his words profitable.

[4] James Montgomery.

ORIGIN OF PRAYER AND SACRIFICE 131

Seneca the Roman, a philosopher in the midst of idolatry, proclaimed God's unity when he prayed: "We worship and adore the framer and former of the Universe; governor, disposer, keeper. Him on whom all things depend; mind and spirit of the world; from whom all things spring; by whose spirit we live. God of all power. God always present. God above all gods. Thee we worship and adore." (Heiler.)

The ancient Mexicans recognized, amid all their cruel idolatries, a Supreme Being and addressed him as "Invisible, without body, One God of perfection and purity under whose wings we find repose and sure defense."

Even among the Hottentots of South Africa, one of the names of the Great Spirit was, "The Father of all our chiefs"; and the Kekchi tribe of Indians prayed: "O Lord our Mother, our Father, Lord of the hills and the valleys." So near and yet so far was their thought from Christ's words, 'Our Father which art in heaven."

Heiler, in his great monograph on prayer, devotes over one hundred pages to the prayer of primitive races, and discusses its cause and motive as well as its form and to whom it is addressed.

The earliest form of prayer is a cry for help. Through all ages and in all lands this is the dominant note of spontaneous prayer.

Men seek for supernatural help for health, for rain, for triumph over their enemies, for daily bread in time of famine.

A well-known Italian scholar in a recent book on prayer looks with disfavor on the evolutionary theory which teaches that prayer is a form of magic or a modification of the tribal excitement in the dance.[5]

"He considers the studies which have been made of the subject from the empirical, comparative, psychological, and philosophical viewpoints, and declares that the bias toward a theory of evolution, which simply leads to the abstract position of deducing a religious act like prayer from an act which is not prayer, is a defect which vitiates practically the whole field of contemporary religious study. Those giving an account of the origin of prayer are influenced by some particular system of thought which forces them to take an *a priori* position. For example, the psychoanalysts concentrate their view on a one-sided interpretation and perceive nothing in prayer but an outlet for sexual excitement."

Professor Tylor in his great work on Primitive Culture suggests that the Tibetan prayer wheel and other methods of charms and spells are degraded survivals of prayer in which original intelligent petitions have dwindled into mystic sentences. If this be true and we admit that prayers may pass into spells, is not the reverse possible and may not prayer have had its origin in magic? No, there is a real distinction which Jevons points out in his chapter on prayer:

"The difference between prayer and spell lies in the difference of the spirit inspiring them; and then we shall see that the difference is essential, fundamental, as little to be ignored as it is impossible to bridge." [6]

[5] Mario Puglisi, *Prayer*, translated by Bernard M. Allen. New York: Macmillan, 1929, p. 296.

[6] Jevons, *Introduction to the Study of Comparative Religion*, p. 152.

Moreover, prayer was prior to magic. It moves in a higher sphere. This is very evident from its very content and aim. As Sidney Dark observes:

"The fact that some phenomena which accompany strong religious emotion are also characteristic of other emotional upheavals (such as anger, love, and so forth) is no evidence that religion is simply one of these other emotions under a slightly perplexing disguise. Yet this also is suggested—to say no more—by some of the popular treatments of religion from the psychological point of view. One might as well say that because a man kneels to prayer, and also to retrieve a collar-stud from beneath a chest of drawers, the former action has no other significance or intention than the latter. Indeed, it is probably only the accident that primitive man did not wear collar-studs which has prevented some irresponsible investigator from finding the origin of kneeling in prayer in this fact." [7]

The use of prayer, moreover, is more universal than magic itself. Prayers of praise are found in ancient India, Egypt, Babylonia, Peru, and Mexico. That is, the ritual of prayer already existed in the earliest civilizations. Primitive prayer, as we shall see later, includes not only self-centered petition but devout confession and requests for pardon. Men express their religious feelings in terms of their own moral standards. The divine image is blurred by their own gross desires. But they express those desires in address to unseen supernatural powers.

"No *a priori* proofs of any cogency, therefore, have been adduced by Dr. Frazer, and none therefore are likely

[7] Sidney Dark, *Orthodoxy Sees It Through*, p. 170.

to be produced by anyone else, to show that there was ever a period in the history of man when prayers and religion were unknown to him. The question remains whether any actual instances are known to the science of religion." [8]

We must therefore refuse to give assent to the opinion of Tylor "that prayer appeared in the religion of the lower culture but that in its earlier stage it was unethical." The examples we give later prove the contrary.

We have definite and beautiful examples of prayer from the Negritos of the Philippine Islands, the Yamema of Tierra del Fuego, the Batwa of Ruanda, and the Bushmen of South Africa. There is but one primitive people among whom we cannot yet prove the existence of prayer, namely, the Andamanese.[9]

According to Heiler, who collected evidences from a wide field, and whose statements are all carefully documented, prayer among primitives is not only individual but also corporate. It is at times therefore formal and follows a ritual with or without accompaniment of sacrifice. At other times it is individual and spontaneous. The content of prayer among primitive tribes—among all those who have a conception of a Sky-god or Highgod includes appeal, complaint, prayer for health, food, crops, children, cattle, victory over enemies, and success in magic.

More rarely we find intercession for wife and chil-

[8] Jevons, *op. cit.*, p. 160.
[9] Schmidt, *Origin and Growth of Religion*, pp. 278, 279.

dren, for friends and, in some cases, even for strangers. Then there are sacrificial formulas and prayers of confession of which we shall speak later.[10]

There is always a special reverence and an attitude of awe in the worshiper, and we must not forget the psychological significance of this fact. The position of the body is not ordinary. Men lift their hands or their arms, they prostrate themselves, take off their sandals or their clothing, they cover or uncover the head; again they use special gestures of invocation or greeting when they pray.[11] All of which is not intended as magic or spell, but evidently is due to the sense of awe and fear in approaching the unseen Spirit whose dwelling place is high above men and whose attributes are not like those of mortals.

Not in every case is prayer addressed to the High-God or the Great Spirit. Alas! most of their prayers are to the spirits of the forest or the sea, to the lesser gods who dwell with men. They also address prayer to idols and fetishes, the local gods who rule their immediate environment. They invoke the aid also of their ancestors or propitiate their spirits by offerings and supplications. Nevertheless the conception of a supreme God is not wholly absent.[12]

Heiler summarizes the significance of primitive prayer as follows:

[10] Heiler, *Das Gebet*, pp. 47-58 and 59-90.
[11] *Ibid.*, pp. 98-109.
[12] *Ibid.*, pp. 131-139.

"Primitive prayer is no soliloquy, no meditation, but a cry to God, a speech with God. Face to face with an 'I' is a 'thou,' with man another manlike being; the 'I' and the 'thou,' man and the other, come into relation with each other. *Prayer is a social phenomenon.*

"The social relation in which the praying man stands to God is one of subordination and dependence. God is greater and mightier than man, man's destiny is in his power. This relation of dependence is always a faithful reflection of an earthly social relation, mostly one of kinship or of subjection. This social relation supporting the prayer is nearly always expressed in the introductory words. 'The idea of the kinship of man with God,' says Dr. Farnell, 'belongs to the alphabet of true prayer.' 'In the liturgies of primitive peoples as of advanced religion the divinity is ordinarily addressed in the relations of kinship.' Aeschylus makes the chorus in the *Suppliants* cry: 'O Mother Earth, O Mother Earth! Turn from us what is terrible! O Father, Son of Earth, Zeus!'

"The relation of the praying man to God as a filial relation is a primitive religious phenomenon. In this address to God, Pygmies and Australians, Bantu-peoples and Indians clasp hands with Greeks, Romans, Assyrians, and Hindus. Primitive men call the Creator and Heavenly Father, the mysterious First Cause, by the name 'Father,' and with this name they address him in prayer. They boast to him of their filial relation. 'Art thou not our father? Are we not thy children?'

"It is true that the name 'father' in many primitive prayers is merely a polite phrase, not the expression of a real filial feeling; frequently the pleasing manner and cordiality in prayer are only half genuine, determined by the selfish effort to prevail upon God. But in many primitive prayers the names 'father' and 'mother' spring from the depths of the soul. In many prayers to ancestors, to

ORIGIN OF PRAYER AND SACRIFICE 137

the life-bestowing goddess, and to the exalted Supreme Father, we find the language of fervor and affection which springs from a real filial relation to the divinity. We must lay aside the modern prejudice that, as Alfred Maury said, 'fear is the father of religion and love its late-born daughter.' The real primitive man is no 'savage,' no 'uncivilized creature,' no half-brute whose only psychical springs of action are fear and self-seeking; 'he is an unspoiled product of Nature of a lovable character.' The attitude which primitive man takes up toward those people whose goodness he knows by experience is the same attitude which he assumes in communicating with supernatural beings. The same affection and trustfulness which he shows toward parents and relations he reveals also in prayer to those exalted beings who are to him as father or mother, grandfather or grandmother. He speaks as a child to his parents. In perfect candor he expresses himself frankly, he 'pours out his heart' in simple confidence—God is no stranger, he knows him well; with unaffected sincerity he loves him because he has often experienced his goodness; with heartfelt confidence he trusts in him, he relies on his power and kindness."[18]

Actual examples of primitive prayer prove the truth of these statements.

A Delaware Indian prayed before going to war: "Great Spirit above! Have pity on my children and on my wife. Let them not mourn for me. Let me succeed in this enterprise, slay mine enemy, return in safety to my dear family and friends that we may rejoice together. Have pity on me and protect my life."

[18] Fredrich Heiler, *Prayer*. A Study in the History and Psychology of Religion. Translated by Samuel McComb, D.D. Pp. 58, 59, 63.

Among the Khonds of Orissa, India, they use this prayer: "O Boorah Penner [the name of their God], who created us and made us to be hungry, who gave us corn and taught us to plow. Remember this and grant our prayers. When we go out in the early morning to sow save us from the tiger and the snake. Let not the birds eat the seed. Let our plows go easily through the earth. Let the corn be plentiful. Let our cattle be so many that there shall be no room for them in the stalls. You know what is good for us. Give it to us."

The following prayer was heard from the lips of an African pagan, a chief among his people: "Mbamba, thou hast held back the rain; give us rain lest we die. Save us from death by famine. Thou art our Father and we are thy children and thou hast created us. Dost thou desire our death? Give us daily food. Thou hast given us legs to run and arms to work and children also. Now give us rain that we may have a harvest."

Nor do pagans pray only for material things. Some of their prayers rise to the ethical and spiritual level and reveal the deeper hunger and famine of the soul. The Gallas of East Africa have an evening prayer that has this beautiful petition: "To Thee, O God, we take our flight; do not take Thy flight and go away from us."

The Kekchi Indians use as a morning prayer words full of pathos: "Who is my Father, Who is my Mother? Only thou, O God, thou seest me and guardest me on all my path, in darkness and trouble. Thou, Lord of the valleys and the mountains."

Most remarkable of all we find even among Pagans of Africa prayers of intercession for others, unselfish prayers. Professor Routledge, who with his wife traveled in East Africa, gives the following prayer offered by a pagan chief in Kikuyu, who was their host:

"O God, accept this offering for the white man who has come to my hut. If the white man or his wife should become ill, may it not be a serious illness. The white man has come from far across the sea to us. He is a good man and treats the people kindly who labor for him. . . . . May they not quarrel with him. . . . Wherever he travels may he not become seriously ill. I am also a good man and a rich man, and we together are as close as if we had had a common mother. O God, here is a fat sheep as an offering for thee which I and the white man and my people offer at the trunk of this tree. Let me not become sick; because I have taught the white man to offer thee, just as if he too were one of the real tribe of Mkikuyu."

Regarding prayer among the Algonquin Indians, Dr. Frank G. Speck gives the first part of the annual thanksgiving ceremony of the Delaware Indians as follows:

"I am thankful, O Thou Great Spirit, that we have been spared to live until now to purify with cedar smoke this our House, because that has always been the rule in the ancient world since the beginning of creation. When anyone thinks of his children, how fortunate it is to see them enjoy good health! And this is the cause of a feeling of happiness, when we consider how greatly we are blessed by the benevolence of our father, the Great Spirit. And we can also feel the great strength of him, our grandfather Fire, to whom we give pleasure when we purify him and take care of him, and when we feed him with this cedar. All of this together we offer in esteem for him, our grandfather, because he has compassion, when he sees how pitifully we behave while we are pleading with all the manitos above, as they were created, and with all those here on earth. Give us everything, our father, that we ask of you, Great Spirit, even the Creator." [14]

John Tanner, who was taken captive by the Indians in 1830 and wrote a narrative of his captivity, tells how the Ottawa Indians invoked the Great Spirit before the beginning of a perilous voyage.

" 'We were passed on,' he writes, 'into the sea about 200 yards, when all the boats halted together, and the chief with a very loud voice addressed a prayer to the Great Spirit, in which he implored him to conduct us safely through the sea. He said, 'Thou hast made this sea, and Thou hast made us Thy children. Thou canst also arrange that the sea remains smooth, whilst we pass on in safety." In this manner he continued to pray through five or ten minutes. Then he threw into the sea a small handful of tobacco, and all of the canoes followed him. They then all continued their voyage, and the old chief began a song of a religious nature.' "

The Arapaho Indians, according to Dr. Schmidt, use a prayer before mealtime. Among the Cheyennes the same custom is in vogue.

---

[14] Publications of the Pennsylvania Historical Commission, vol. ii, p. 82. Harrisburg, 1931.

ORIGIN OF PRAYER AND SACRIFICE

"A meal was begun and finished with prayer, and before eating, a little of (the contents of) every kettle was offered to the Manitus: the food was elevated toward heaven and then put on the soil at the corner of the fire. Many prayers were performed in the healing ceremony executed by the medicine-man, who had received his power from the Supreme Being. A special prayer was recited and a song sung on the death of a person of some importance, over the corpse of the dead." [15]

Before we pass on to the origin of sacrifice, it may be well to give one of the sacrificial prayers used by the Chinese Emperor at the service formerly performed in the Temple of Heaven twice each year:

"Thou hast vouchsafed, O God, to hear us, for Thou as our Father dost regard us. I, Thy child, dull and unenlightened, am unable to show forth my feelings. Honorable is Thy great name. With reverence we spread out these precious stores and silk, and as swallows rejoicing in the Spring praise Thine abundant love. The great and lofty One sends down His favor and regard, which we, in our insignificance, are hardly sufficient to receive. I, His simple servant, while I worship, present this precious cup to Him whose years have no end. Men and creatures are emparadised, O God, in Thy love. All living things are indebted to Thy goodness, but who knows whence his blessings come to him? It is Thou alone, O Lord, who art the true parent of all things. The service is completed, but our poor sincerity cannot be fully expressed. Thy sovereign goodness is indefinite. As a potter hast Thou made all living things. Great and small are curtained round by Thee. As engraven on the heart of Thy poor servant is the sense of Thy goodness, but my feeling can-

[15] Schmidt, *High Gods in America*.

not be fully displayed. With great kindness dost Thou bear with us, and notwithstanding our demerits dost grant us life and prosperity. Spirits and men rejoice together, praising God the Lord. What limit, what measure can there be, while we celebrate His great name? Forever He setteth fast the high heavens, and shapeth the solid earth. His government is everlasting. His poor servant, I bow my head and lay it in the dust, bathed in His grace and glory. We have worshiped and written the great name on this gemlike sheet. Now we display it before God, and place it in the fire. These valuable offerings of silks and fine meats we burn also, with these sincere prayers, that they may ascend in volumes of flames up to the distant azure. All the ends of the earth look up to Him. All human beings, all things on the earth, rejoice together in the Great Name." [16]

What was the origin of sacrifice?

To those who accept the Scriptures as the word of God the answer is evident and all explanations of totemism and sympathetic magic seem far-fetched and fantastic. "It has yet to be proved," says E. O. James, President of the Folklore Society of Great Britain, "that the Hebrews passed through a totemic stage in the evolution of their highly complex sacrificial system. Be this as it may, it certainly cannot now be maintained that 'originally all sacrifices were eaten by the worshipers,' and, 'in the oldest sacrifice the blood was drunk by the worshipers, and after it ceased to be it was poured out upon the altar.' "[17]

---
[16] Charles H. Robinson, D.D., *The Interpretation of the Character of Christ to Non-Christian Races*, p. 194.
[17] E. O. James, *Origins of Sacrifice*, p. 47.

In this volume from which we have quoted James gives a detailed and critical analysis of the origin and history of sacrifice in religion. The standpoint of the author is indicated in his preface:

"In the anthropological treatment of a ritual of this character, which has persisted throughout the ages, and undergone a complete metamorphosis in the long course of its complex history, there is a danger of interpreting the final products in terms of crude beginnings, by the simple method of overleaping the intervening series of changes in thought and expression. As Professor Percy Gardner has pointed out, it is all too easy to assume, for example, that the notion of a ceremonial eating of a divine victim persisted from savage orgiastic rites, not only into the more civilized pagan mysteries, but even into early Christianity. A certain school of anthropologists, he says, take ancient religion at its lowest, not at its highest levels, regardless of the fact that 'while magic and materialism no doubt persisted, all the noble spirits warred against them.' The author believes, with Dr. Westermarck, that the idea of substitution is vital in blood sacrifices. In this practice of offering life to preserve life may be discerned the beginnings of the idea of substitution and propitiation, which, in many of the higher religions, have taken over a lofty ethical significance."

The blood was regarded as the life-stream, the very seat of vitality being the heart. This is the fundamental belief, expressed in Scripture language, that "the blood is the life" and that blood makes atonement, an idea which we find perhaps even in the Paleolithic age. Clemen refers to it in his book on the *Religion of the Stone Age,* and James speaks of the cave paintings in France:

"Thus, for example, in the inner recesses of the cavern called Niaux, near Tarascon-en-Ariège, three hollows on the ground have been utilized as wounds by drawing around them the outline of a bison, and annexing to the cups little arrows painted in red. It is now generally admitted that designs of this character, which are numerous in the Franco-Cantabrian region, together with the mutilated clay models of animals having spear thrusts upon them, recently discovered by M. Casteret at Montespan, can only be explained satisfactorily in terms of hunting magic. Nothing less than a strong supernatural reason is likely to have led Magdalenian man into a cave which today necessitates swimming nearly a mile up a subterranean stream, and passing through the neck of a syphon—if these conditions prevailed in Paleolithic times." [18]

But we do not need to go back to the Stone Age and the uncertain interpretation of archaeological discoveries. Dr. Ross devotes an entire chapter to sacrifice in primitive Chinese faith. The significance of sacrifice in China he defines as follows: Sacrifice may be offered in order to obtain one or more of four objects: (1) the offering may be propitiatory, intended to appease the anger or to avert the judgment of Deity, who is believed to be offended by some wrongdoing on the part of the offerer; (2) it may be reverential, expressive of honor; (3) it may be donative, in acknowledgment of, and gratitude for, favors received; (4) it may be implorative, to secure favors in the future,

[18] James, *op. cit.,* pp. 23, 24.

ORIGIN OF PRAYER AND SACRIFICE

either (a) by averting impending calamity, or (b) by obtaining blessings, spiritual, physical, personal, or relative. Sacrifice implies a sense on the part of the offerer both of dependence and of need.[19]

This general division of sacrifice applies in general to all primitive tribes. It can be put into tabular form as follows:

I. *Communal Sacrifice:*
   A festal meal with or without a slain victim.
   As pledge of kinship with the gods. Here the gods are regarded as kin.

II. *Honorific Sacrifice:*
   a) Periodical gifts of honor to gods.
   b) Emergency gifts (for rain, etc.).
   The gods considered as rulers who need to be honored.

III. *Piacular Sacrifice for Propitiation:*
   The gods as estranged or angry.
   Blood sacrifice.
   Hair offering (as part of victim).
   Salt covenant (salt = blood).

Thus, we have in primitive sacrifice the threefold idea of fellowship, gratitude, and propitiation with a sense of sin or unworthiness.

All of these are not found among all primitives, yet there are clear examples of each form in many far separated cultures, e.g., the Eskimo, the Pygmies, the Algonquins, the Bushmen, and the Veddas.[20] The dominant form is the offering of first-fruits or por-

[19] *The Original Religion of China*, p. 106.
[20] Schmidt, *Origin and Growth of Religion*, p. 280.

tions of the food; in the case of hunting tribes the offering of the skulls or the marrow-bones obtained in the chase. One pygmy tribe has a sin-offering of a sort without parallel in the world. The Semang of Malacca, during thunder storms, say that it is the voice of their Supreme Being, Kari; then they take a bamboo knife, make a little cut with it at the knee, mix the blood with water, and throw the mixture skyward, praying at the same time for pardon, and if the storm lasts, making a detailed confession of their sins.[21] Regarding the Isoka Tribe in Nigeria, we read that ancestors are worshiped on various occasions, but

"most of all they are worshiped and expiatory sacrifices offered when the family name has been sullied by incest, adultery, theft, or misuse of the family land and possessions. Should the priest advise that a sickness is caused by an ancestor, members of the family are urged to confess any sins they have committed, and sacrifices are offered."[22]

In view of all this evidence, the whole idea that the origin of sacrifice is due to Totemism can no longer be sustained, although it had as its distinguished protagonist W. Robertson Smith.[23]

Le Roy defines Totemism as follows:

"An institution consisting essentially of a magical pact, representing and forming a relationship of a mystical and supernatural order, by which, under the visible form of

[21] Schmidt, *op. cit.*, p. 281.
[22] Welch, "The Isoka Tribe," in *Africa*.
[23] *Religion of the Semites* and *Kinship and Marriage in Early Arabia*.

ORIGIN OF PRAYER AND SACRIFICE

an animal and, by exception, of a vegetable, mineral, or astral body, an invisible spirit is associated with an individual, a family, a clan, a tribe, a secret society, in view of a reciprocity of services."

Then he goes on to say:

"Totemism is a means employed by primitive man to unite, distinguish, strengthen, and extend the family through a magical pact.

"It *creates* neither the religious conscience nor morality nor belief in spirits nor sacrifice nor communion: on the contrary, *it supposes all these as already existing,* and uses them to perpetuate itself. To make an alliance with an invisible being, it is necessary to believe that it exists: you do not ally yourself with nothing.

"It is, then, not the primitive religion, it is not even a religion nor even a part of religion. It is a family and social magical pact." [24]

In his latest work on *Semitic and Hamitic Origins,* George A. Barton of the University of Pennsylvania retracts his earlier opinions and repudiates them. *The Semites were not totemistic;* the facts collected by W. R. Smith must, he says, be explained in some other way.[25]

They can be explained in the best and easiest way by opening our Bibles at Gen. 3: 21: "And Jehovah God made for Adam and for his wife coats of skins and clothed them." Archbishop Trench, preaching on that text in Westminster Abbey, years ago, said:

"We note in this Scripture that the clothing which God

[24] Le Roy, *The Religion of the Primitives,* p. 87.
[25] *Semitic and Hamitic Origins,* pp. 123, 218 ff.

found for Adam could only have been obtained at the cost of a life, and *that* the life of one unguilty, of one who had no share nor part in the sin which made the providing of it needful. So it must necessarily have been. A beast, one or more, must have been slain before these coats of skins could have been prepared; and it must have been slain by the act of God. I do not scruple to say that we have here the first institution of sacrifice; and what is more noticeable still, God himself the institutor; not merely enjoining, commanding, but himself ordaining, showing the way; and the central idea of sacrifice, as it afterward unfolded itself in mainfold rites, is wrapped up in this first idea of Paradise."

Surely the mention of an occurrence so apparently trivial in the midst of a solemn history must have arisen from its association with some other transaction of higher importance, and that was none else than the institution of animal sacrifices, an institution undoubtedly of Divine appointment, adapted to the capabilities of men in early ages, and designed to transmit the instruction given as to the only acceptable mode of worship for sinful creatures, by faith in a Redeemer, through the medium of a symbolical rite, which impressively reminded them of that fundamental truth. The fig-leaf aprons were of no use either as an adequate or a permanent covering; and, besides, they stirred no recollections, nor suggested any needful cheering thoughts. Whereas, the skin of a lamb or a kid, besides being more durable, could not be procured without the death of the animal; and as its slaughter, if effected by the hands of the first man, must have been a substitutionary victim, to be offered according to the Divine directions, the blood-stained hide of the slain beast, as it was worn on the persons of the fallen pair, would be a constant painful remembrance of the death which their guilt deserved. The mention of the "coats of skin," then, as Archbishop Trench and other commentators suggest, is eminently worthy, considering their origin and their use, of the place it holds among the momentous details of this tragic narrative. They are associated with the institution of a sacred rite of deep symbolical import; and certainly no time could have been more seasonable— rather, none could have been so appropriate—for the appointment of that rite, and the supply of that clothing, as when the announcement of the Redeemer was first made, when the need of his propitiatory death began to be felt, and the benefits of being clad in the robes of his righteousness were held out to man. There was a subordinate object served by the furnishing of those skins. "By this clothing," says Kiel, "God imparted to the feeling of shame the visible sign of an awakened conscience, and to the consequent necessity for a covering to the bodily nakedness, the higher work of a suitable discipline for the sinner." By selecting the skins of beasts for the clothing of the first pair, and therefore causing the death or slaughter of beasts for that purpose, he showed them how they might use the sovereignty they possessed over the animals for their own good, and even sacrifice animal life for the preservation of human; so that this act of God laid the foundation for the sacrifices, even if the first clothing did not prefigure our ultimate "clothing upon" (II Cor. 5: 4), nor the coats of skin the robe of righteousness.[26]

[26] Cf. Jamieson, Fausset, and Brown, *Critical and Experimental Commentary,* Genesis, p. 61.

CHAPTER SIX

THE ORIGIN OF FIRE-WORSHIP AND FIRE AS A SYMBOL OF DEITY

THE fire thus brought from a burning ground is then fed with fuel and is placed on a piece of ground open to wind. By its side and in a windward direction, they place a heap of powdered sandalwood, frankincense, and such other easily combustible substances. The heat and the blaze of the fire, carried by the wind toward the heap, ignites it. When thus ignited, this fresh fire is fed with fuel. Then, again, by its side another heap of powdered sandalwood, frankincense, and such other combustibles is placed in such a position that the blaze and the heat of the fire produced as above may be carried by the wind toward it and that it may be easily ignited. This process is repeated ninety-one times. The distance between each burning fire and the next heap to be ignited must be about half a *gaz* or about a foot. Each preceding fire is allowed to extinguish itself. The fire ignited for the ninety-first time is then considered to be fit for use and is kept burning by being regularly fed. This is the process of collecting the first fire in the above list of sixteen fires, *viz.*, the fire of a burning corpse."

JIVANJI JAMSHEDJI MODI,
in THE RELIGIOUS CEREMO-
NIES AND CUSTOMS OF THE
PARSEES, *p. 214.*

CHAPTER SIX

THE ORIGIN OF FIRE-WORSHIP AND FIRE AS A SYMBOL OF DEITY

FROM THE EARLIEST AGES AND IN EVERY PART OF the world man has associated fire with worship. The smoke of an altar, the cloud of incense, and the burning of a flame are met with on the threshold of religion. Long before it was recorded in Holy Writ men have whispered: "Our God is a consuming fire."

Fire-worship was one of the earliest forms of approach to the unseen gods, and the origin of fire is one of the mysteries of early civilization, which only finds its key in the Scriptures.

A. E. Crawley says in the "Encyclopedia of Religion and Ethics" (Vol. VI, p. 28) that "the mention of fire and the fire ritual is remarkably rare in the Hebrew books, although the principle and practice of burnt-offering are ubiquitous." Quite the contrary is the fact. The Old and New Testaments contain more than four hundred references to fire, its use on the altar or as a symbol for the presence of God and his manifestation in power or in judgment. The worship of Ra, the Sun-god of Egypt, that of Agni the Fire-god of India, that of fire as symbol of deity by the Zoroastrians—all this may be only a dim recollection on the part of the scattered race of that terrible scene at the gates of a lost Paradise when the cherubim with flaming sword guarded the way to the Tree of Life. From central Mexico to the far South Seas and to northern Japan, as we shall see, there are evidences of fire-worship.

Abel's offering was doubtless accepted by fire. Of Abraham we read that when Jehovah made covenant with him "it came to pass when the sun went down and it was dark, behold a smoking furnace and a flaming torch" passed between the divided sacrificial offering, and the horror of a great darkness fell upon Abraham.[1] Moses first heard Jehovah's voice at the burning bush in the desert of Midian. Again at Sinai "the sight of the glory of the Lord was like a devouring fire on the top of the mount in the eyes of the children of Israel."[2] The pillar of fire and the cloud by day were the symbol of the presence of Jehovah for forty years with Israel in the wilderness. Gideon's sacrifice was kindled by the touch of an angel.[3] In the Tabernacle and in the Temple the golden candlestick sent forth its light perpetually in the holy of holies, while the smoke and fire of incense and sacrifice were the constant symbols of worship.

Fire came down from heaven in blessing and in

[1] Gen. 15: 12-17.
[2] Exod. 24: 17.
[3] Judges 6: 21.

THE ORIGIN OF FIRE-WORSHIP 155

judgment. On the threshing-floor of Ornan, where David built his altar;[4] on Mount Carmel and Mount Horeb to Elijah; to Solomon at the dedication of the Temple;[5] and in the judgment of those who defied the prophet Elijah.[6]

Isaiah received in vision a coal from the Divine altar to purge his lips and recorded the promise: "The Light of Israel will become a fire and his holy one a flame .... to burn and devour his thorns and briars in one day."[7] Ezekiel's great vision of the presence of Jehovah is in whirling wheels of flame and a light inaccessible and full of glory.

Jesus Christ came to baptize with fire. "I am come to cast fire on the earth."[8] While in the last portrait of our Savior, John sees him, his face as the sun shining in strength, with eyes as a flame of fire, his feet as brass burning in a furnace, and walking amid the seven burning golden candlesticks and seven stars in his right hand. The tongues of flame at Pentecost and "the seven lamps of fire burning before the throne" are the sevenfold Spirit of God. So full is the Bible of this one great symbol that it might well be called the Book of Divine Fire. In type and promise and symbolism and theophany our God is a consuming fire. No wonder the universal Church sings:

[4] I Chron. 21 : 26.
[5] II Chron. 7 : 1.
[6] II Kings 1 : 10-12.
[7] Isa. 10 : 17.
[8] Luke 12 : 49.

"Come, Holy Ghost, our souls inspire,
And lighten with celestial fire.
Thou the anointing Spirit art,
Who dost thy sevenfold gifts impart."

And so God's ministers themselves become flames of fire.[9] Fire is regarded in the Scriptures as one of the agents of the Divine will and a concomitant of various theophanies (Gen. 15: 17; Exod. 3: 2; Deut. 4: 36; Ps. 78: 14). Fire is also the instrument of divine wrath (Num. 11: 1; Deut. 32: 22; Amos 1: 4; Isa. 65: 5), but God himself is not in the fire; it is only his symbol (I King 19: 12).

According to a Rabbinical legend, fire was created on the eve of the Sabbath when Adam, overwhelmed by the darkness, feared that this too was a consequence of his sin. "Whereupon the Holy One put in his way two bricks which he rubbed against each other and from which fire came forth."[10] The Torah given by God was made of "an integument of white fire, the engraved letters were of black fire, and it was itself of fire mixed with fire, hewn out of fire, and given from the midst of fire."[11]

So much for the place of fire in the Scriptures and in Jewish tradition. When we consider its place in primitive religion and in the great ethnic faiths, we find so many strange parallels that they seem to point to a common and primary origin.

[9] Heb. 1: 6.
[10] "Jewish Encyclopedia," article Fire (Yer. Ber., 12a).
[11] *Ibid.* (Yer. Sotak, VIII: 22).

THE ORIGIN OF FIRE-WORSHIP 157

Tylor, in his great work on *Primitive Culture*, says:

"The real and absolute worship of fire falls into two great divisions, the first belonging rather to fetishism, the second to polytheism proper, and the two apparently representing an earlier and later stage of theological ideas. The first is the rude barbarian's adoration of the actual flame which he watches writhing, roaring, devouring like a live animal; the second belongs to an advanced generalization, that any individual fire is a manifestation of one general elemental being—the Fire-god. Unfortunately, evidence of the exact meaning of fire-worship among the lower races is scanty, while the transition from fetishism to polytheism seems a gradual process of which the stages elude close definition. Moreover, it must be borne in mind that rites performed with fire are, though often, yet by no means necessarily, due to worship of the fire itself. Authors who indiscriminately mixed up such rites as the new fire, the perpetual fire, the passing through the fire, classing them as acts of fire-worship, without proper evidence as to their meaning in any particular case, have added to the perplexity of a subject not too easy to deal with, even under strict precautions. Two sources of error are especially to be noted. On the one hand, fire happens to be a usual means whereby sacrifices are transmitted to departed souls and deities in general; and on the other hand, the ceremonies of earthly fire-worship are habitually and naturally transferred to celestial fire-worship in the religion of the Sun." [12]

To avoid these sources of error we will treat first of the origin of fire in human culture, then of fire as a symbol of deity, lastly as a way of communion with deity and as a symbol of Divine favor.

[12] Edward B. Tylor, *Primitive Culture*, vol. ii, pp. 277, 278.

THE ORIGIN OF FIRE-WORSHIP

1. The use of fire as an agent in human culture goes back to prehistoric ages. From time to time travelers have told about fireless peoples. But all these stories have long since been proved without foundation. No one knows who invented fire. Its use and preservation is absolutely universal. "FIRE, GREATEST OF ALL DISCOVERIES, ENABLING MAN TO LIVE IN VARIOUS CLIMATES, USE MANY FOODS, AND COMPEL THE FORCES OF NATURE TO DO HIS WORK." [13]

Recent scientific speculation places the knowledge of fire-making as early as the Second Interglacial period, approximately 400,000 years ago! In all likelihood the first suggestion came neither from volcanic fire nor from lightning, but from the inevitable sparks produced in the early manufacture of flint arrows and implements.[14] The primitive methods of fire-making are by friction, percussion, or compression. The modern method is chemical. The stick and groove method was used chiefly in the South Sea Islands. The fire-drill and the fire-saw have a much wider range in Australia, Tasmania, ancient India, Europe, Africa, and North and South America. In Borneo, Sumatra, and parts of eastern Asia, fire was occasionally made by striking two pieces of split bamboo together. Flints were used in the Paleolithic age and by the Eskimos and the North American Indians. "But there does not seem to be

---

[13] Part of the inscription on the Union Station, Washington, D. C.

[14] "Encyclopedia of Religion and Ethics," vol. vi, p. 26. Article, Fire and Fire-gods.

THE ORIGIN OF FIRE-WORSHIP

any regular course of evolution in fire-making methods," says Crawley. Therefore the myths regarding its origin are widespread and numerous. All seem agreed that fire is a gift of the gods. Each nation has its own story of a Prometheus.

In China they tell of "a great sage who went to walk beyond the bounds of the moon and the sun; he saw a tree and on this tree a bird which pecked at it and made fire come forth. The sage was struck with this, took a branch of the tree, and produced fire from it." Hence he was called Sun-jin-she, i.e., the first person who produced fire.[15] The Sanskrit name for the fire-spindle used in making fire is *pramantha*, which is probably connected with the name of the Greek fire-giver Prometheus.[16]

Agni (Latin *ignis*, fire) is the first word of the first hymn of the Rig Veda. "Agni, I entreat, divine appointed priest of sacrifice." No god stands higher than Agni the fire-god, mighty in his power, yet lowly in his ministry to man as the protector of the family hearth.[17] "No origin myths," says Walter Hough, "yield so much interest as those relating to the manner in which fire came to man." They are found among American Indians, in Polynesia, in Oceania, and among African and Asiatic races. Throughout the world there appears a similarity. Prometheus steals fire from heaven; the Coyote of North America steals it from

[15] E. B. Tylor, *Early History of Mankind*, p. 256.
[16] A. Kuhn, *Die Herabkunft des Feuers*, Gütersloh, 1886, pp. 13-15.
[17] Tylor, *Primitive Culture*, vol. ii, p. 281.

an old woman. Here are a few out of hundreds of examples:[18]

"The Maidu fire myth recounts that after the people had found fire Thunder seized it away from them and kept it for himself under the care of a little bird. The people were thus compelled to resume the conditions of primitive times, but succeeded in stealing the fire by strategy of Mouse, Deer, Dog, Coyote, and Skunk. The Mouse crept in Thunder's lodge, placed fire in a flute, a portion in Dog's ear, and some on the hock of Deer's leg, and raced back pursued by Thunder.

"The fire-origin myth of the Eskimo of Kegitareik is as follows: After the creation of the coast men, who were born from a bean pod, Raven taught them how to live. 'He taught them how to make a fire drill and bow from a piece of dry wood and a cord, taking the wood from the bushes and small trees he had caused to grow in hollows and sheltered places on the hillsides.' He returned then and taught the first man who lived inland 'to make fire with a fire drill and place the spark of tinder in a bunch of dry grass and wave it about until it blazed, and then to place dry wood upon it. Also to roast fish on a stick.'

"The Uintah Utes say: 'Coyote caught fire and gave it to the Indians. The Indians kept the fire and never lost it again. It made light and heat. It was cold; and if there had been no fire the Indians would all have died. The fire kept them alive. Coyote said, "It is very good to do that." He gave life to the Indians. Perhaps Coyote got the fire from the white men in the east.'"

The Maori of New Zealand say that fire was derived from the fire children born of the Dawn Maid

[18] Walter Hough, *Fire as an Agent in Human Culture*, Smithsonian Institution, Washington, D. C., 1926, pp. 156-164.

THE ORIGIN OF FIRE-WORSHIP 161

and named for the five fingers of the hand. In Ceylon the "story current about the blue-black swallow-tailed flycatcher, and its mortal enemy, the crow, is that the former, like Prometheus of old, brought down fire from heaven for the benefit of man. The crow, jealous of the honor, dipped his wings in water and shook the drippings over the flame, quenching it. Since that time there has been deadly enmity between the birds."

According to Junod, the southern Bantus have the following myth:

"In the Ronga clans these two ancestors of mankind are called Likala Humba and Nsilambowa. The first name means the one who brought a glowing cinder in a shell, viz., the originator of fire. Nsilambowa, the name of the woman, means the one who grinds vegetables. The first human beings, according to these names, would have been those who introduced fire and the culinary art into the world! This idea is interesting, and seems to show that for the native mind the cooking of food is the pursuit which differentiates man from the animals." [19]

The Sioux Indians in their ghost dance have a song that carries back the origin of fire, not to our first ancestors, but to God himself:

"It was the Father who gave us these things,
It was the Father who gave us these things,
It was the Father who gave us fire,
It was the Father who gave us fire,
The Father gave it to us,
The Father gave it to us."

[19] H. A. Junod, *The Life of a South African Tribe*, vol. ii, p. 327.

The significance of all these myths and traditions is obvious. Fire is from above. It is a gift of the gods. Its use distinguishes man from the brute creation. Its invention or discovery gave him lordship and power. It is not surprising, therefore, that we find fire-worship and fire-ritual widely diffused.

2. Fire is the symbol of deity, not only in certain Ethnic religions, but among savage tribes. There is an extensive pantheon of fire-gods extending from Baal, the Chaldean and Phoenician fire-god, to Mexico's fire-god, with many strange names signifying "Lord of comets," "yellow-face," "the ancient father-god," etc. Bernardino Sahagun gives the following prayer offered to the Mexican fire-god:

"You, Lord, who are the father and mother of gods and the most ancient divinity, know that comes here your vassal, your slave; weeping, he approaches with great sadness; he comes plunged in grief, because he recognizes that he is plunged in error, having slipped over some wicked sins and some grave delinquencies which merit death; he comes, on account of this, very heavy and oppressed. Our god of pity, who art the sustainer and defender of all, receive in penitence and relieve in his anguish your serf and vassal." [20]

The Pueblo Indians also have their fire-god who is represented as "black spotted with red" and a fearsome being; likewise the Navahoes, the Manitous, and the other Algonquin tribes.

The Ainus of northern Japan make much of the fire-

[20] Hough, *op. cit.*, p. 127.

THE ORIGIN OF FIRE-WORSHIP

goddess who is closely connected with their fire-ritual. The missionary Rev. John Bachelor writes:

"The deity who is generally looked upon as standing next in order to the goddess of the sun is the goddess of fire. She is conceived of as being both useful and awful; useful, inasmuch as she warms the body, heals it when ill, and cooks its food; awful, inasmuch as she is a special witness to note the acts and words of men and women. It is she who will appear either for or against us at the Judgment Day. She will present the great Judge of all with a perfect picture of every word and action of each individual human being, and there can be no avoiding her. Thus every person will be rewarded or punished hereafter according to the representations of the goddess of fire. We can, therefore, easily understand the great importance the Ainu attach to fire worship. But here again we must be careful not to think that it is the fire itself which is worshiped. Fire is not worshiped, but a goddess who is supposed to dwell in the fire, and whose vehicle the fire is supposed to be. This is a subtle distinction, but is nevertheless true.

"The Ainu always pray to the goddess of fire in cases of distress. Thus, when a person is taken ill, his friend or relative, the chief of the village gets a new piece of willow wood fresh from the forest, and sitting down before the fire peels off the outer rind and shaves the stick into an *inao*. When it is finished he places it in the corner of the hearth near the fire, and asks the fire goddess, who is supposed to be a great purifier from disease, to look kindly upon the sick one." [21]

According to Schmidt, there is a whole series of races "among whom the Supreme Being is described as 'shining

[21] *The Ainu of Japan*, New York, 193, pp. 277, 97.

white' or 'like fire'; for example, among the Northwestern Semang, the Southern Andamanese, the Wiyot and Patwin of North Central California, the Lenape, and Algonquin tribe, and the Winnebago, a Sioux tribe influenced by the Algonquins. Among the Maidu of North Central California we are assured that the whole form of the Supreme Being shines like the light of the sun, but that his face is always covered and no one has ever seen it, except the Evil Spirit, who did so once. The Kurnai and Wiradyuri teach that the Supreme Being is surrounded by an aureole of sunrays. Among the Samoyeds a shaman saw him blazing with so bright a light that he could not look at him." [22]

The Damaras of South Africa also have a well-developed fire-ritual somewhat similar to that of the Vestal virgins in Rome. The idea of fire as a purifier is universal. One of the best illustrations is that given by Willoughby regarding the Bantu of South Africa:

"Fire often figures in the ritual of expurgation. Some tribes hold that nothing but fire will purge the more personal possessions of the dead. 'Fire was used (by the Basuto) to purify a person who had defiled himself by walking over a grave, or even having his foot upon it. A small fire was lighted and the feet of the person were singed in the flame.' When a Barozi burial-party returns to the village, a small fire is made on the path outside, and the whole party (men and women) have to leap over the fire as a form of purification. The Alunda of Barotseland do not leap over the fire as the Barotse do, but stand at the nearest bifurcation of the path leading to the village, and the oldest woman of the village brings burning sticks and passes them round the burial party. Tumbuka mourn-

[22] *The Origin and Growth of Religion*, p. 266.

THE ORIGIN OF FIRE-WORSHIP 165

ers returning from the grave to the village are met on the path by a 'doctor,' who kindles a great fire and puts certain roots into it, and each of the mourners passes through the flames of the fire. 'To the Central African the hearth and its fires are sacred. For instance, if any serious disease breaks out in a village, the head-man will call upon the medicine-man to place medicine at the crossroads, the village fires are raked out, and the smouldering embers thrown upon the bowl of medicine at the crossroads. All shout aloud and make as much noise as possible, while the medicine-man departs alone to produce a new flame with his fire-stick, from which all fires are rekindled.' " [23]

Sun-worship is closely allied to fire-worship among primitives, especially among the American Indians. On Vancouver Island they prayed to the sun as he mounts the zenith; among the Delawares they sacrificed to the sun; the Virginian Indians bowed before the sun as he rose and set; his likeness is found in the Algonquin picture-writings as representing the Highgod or Great Manitu. The Sioux Indians venerated the Sun as the Maker and Preserver of all things, while the Creeks regarded him as the symbol of the Great Spirit.[24]

It is in the ancient religions of Persia, India, China, and Rome that we have the best examples of fire as symbol of deity, especially in the two lands first named. Zarathustra (Zoroaster) came to a people holding the ancient nature-worship. Their gods were Sky and Earth, Sun and Moon, Fire and Wind. He preached

[23] W. C. Willoughby, *Nature-Worship and Taboo* (Hartford, 1932), pp. 203, 204.

[24] Tylor, *op. cit.*, vol. ii, p. 287.

a spiritual monotheism, the Wise Lord, Ahura Mazda. But the Parsi religion retained its old fire-ritual, described with such sympathy by Dr. Moulton:

"Two buildings are required as soon as a Parsi community of sufficient size is established in any new place— a Fire-temple for the living, and a Tower of Silence for the dead. Let us begin with these, and first with the temple, served by the priests of the higher order, the Mobeds, described in the preceding chapter.

"There are three kinds of Fire-temples. The specially holy place is called an Atesh Behram, a name which combines those of the Avestan Yazads Fire and Victory (*Atar*, Ταραθραγγα). The Indian name Agiari (cf. Vedic Agni = *Ignis*) is a general term usually applied to both the other kinds, *Atesh Adaran* and *Atesh Dadgah*. The difference lies, as we shall see, in the amount of purification the Fire has undergone. A native Iranian name is also used, *Dar-i-Mihr*, or 'Gate of Mithra.' The buildings, which are often not easily distinguishable from an ordinary dwelling-house, are studiously plain and unpretentious; one almost suspects that they eschew ornament of set purpose. All is concentrated on the Fire.

"It is the preparation of the Fire that makes the establishment of an Atesh Behram so costly. The fire has to be compounded of sixteen different fires, all purified after a long and complicated ritual. One of them is the fire from the burning of a corpse, which for a Parsi mind is the last indignity that can be offered to their sacramental element. A number of sandalwood logs are kindled from the cremation. Then above the flame, a little too high to touch it, a metal spoon is held, with small holes in it, containing chips of sandalwood. When these ignite, the flame is made to kindle a fresh fire. This process is repeated ninety-one times, to the accompaniment of recited prayers. The puri-

THE ORIGIN OF FIRE-WORSHIP

fied fire is set aside in an urn, and of course kept burning with special care.

"It is, however, very misleading to use the word 'worship' to describe the attitude of Parsis toward their sacred symbol. If it is held to imply that they regard Fire as a deity, the term is wholly false, though there may be ignorant members of the community who misinterpret the reverence paid to it. Educated Parsis always protest vehemently that for them there is one God, and that reverence offered to angels and spirits, and to the sacramental element, is only a form of approach to the 'Wise Lord.'" [25]

Some say that the history of religion practically includes only two genuine fire-gods: Agni of early Hinduism and Atar of Zoroastrianism. In other cases fire is rather a symbol or a mode of approach to the Divine. The two chief differences, however, between Indian and Persian fire-worship are (1) the abhorrence in the latter of burning the dead, so common among Hindus, and (2) the imperfect personification of Atar as compared with Agni.

Fire in the Brahman religion is the first or primal element produced from Brahma himself. The Upanishads speak of the seven tongues of fire. Sparks and fire resemble each other even as the individual souls of men resemble Brahma. The process of kindling fire with two sticks is an act of generation.

Each morning the family assembled around the hearth saying: "We approach thee, O Fire, with reverence and adoration." The god Agni takes preced-

[25] James Hope Moulton, *The Treasure of the Magi* (Oxford, 1917), pp. 141, 142, 146.

ence over all other gods in sacrifice. His triple form is terrestrial, celestial, and solar fire. He is the giver of immortality and purges from sin. After death he burns away the guilt of the body and carries the immortal part to heaven.[26] How many resemblances we find here to the teaching of the Bible regarding fire as symbol of God's holiness and power to purify the unclean and the sinful!

In China we have no fire-god, but the rotation of nature, the system of cosmogony, is based on the *Yang* and the *Yin*, the light and the dark hemispheres of the universe. The progress of Yang in springtime is characterized by the flowering of the peach-tree. The red brilliant colors of its blossoms represent the destruction of dark and cold winter. Red paper, red firecrackers, bonfires, and torches are therefore used everywhere in China as protection against evil. Fires are lit at the New Year festival to make it propitious.[27] Fire and light and red colors all are hostile to the kingdom of darkness and the specters of the night. Here again we have a faint echo of the words, "God is light. .... God is a consuming fire. ..... In him is no darkness at all."

According to Dr. Clifford H. Plopper, however, popular religion in China has a real fire-god. He is called Chu Yung, or the Red Emperor. He is represented as having the body of an animal, but a human face. His face, beard, and clothing are red. He is a fierce, quick-

[26] "Encyclopedia of Religion and Ethics," vol. vi, p. 29.
[27] De Groot, *The Religion of the Chinese*, pp. 37-39.

THE ORIGIN OF FIRE-WORSHIP

tempered god, delighting in punishing people and sent from heaven for that purpose. His festival takes place on the fifteenth day of the fourth month. Then incense is burned in the home before the kitchen-god and public parades are held in honor of the fire-god.[28]

The Yezdis of Mesopotamia who live near Mosul have, as part of their strange and ancient religion, fire-worship which may be allied to that of the Persians before Islam. Layard says:

"They have more in common with the Sabaeans than with any other sect . . . . reverence the sun . . . . have a temple and oxen dedicated to the sun . . . . kiss the object on which its first beams fall. For fire, as symbolical, they have nearly the same reverence; they never spit into it, but frequently pass their hands through the flame; kiss them and rub them over their right eyebrow, or sometimes over the whole face."

He also says of the priests, who are occupants of the tomb of Sheikh Adi, founder of the sect:

"As servants of Sheikh Adi they are the guardians of his tomb, keep up the holy fires and bring provisions and fuel to those who dwell within its precincts and to pilgrims of distinction." [29]

As another example of the world-wide cult of fire as symbol of deity we have Rome with its Vestal virgins, who kept the perpetual altar-fire burning in

---

[28] *Chinese Religion through Its Proverbs* (Shanghai, 1926), pp. 43, 44.

[29] Hough, *Fire as an Agent in Human Culture*, p. 131.

their sacred temple, and the Greek-Roman legends regarding Prometheus, who brought fire from heaven.

"What was their tale of someone on a summit
  Looking, I think, upon the endless sea—
One with a fate, and sworn to overcome it,
  One who was fettered and who should be free?

"Round him a robe, for shaming and for searing,
  Ate with empoisonment and stung with fire,
He thro' it all was to his lord uprearing
  Desperate patience of a brave desire."

On this legend Aeschylus based his great tragedy *Prometheus Bound*—so full of parallels to Bible teaching.

"Among the Romans," said St. Augustine, "nothing is held more holy than the temple of Vesta."[30] The origin of the Vestal virgins as an organized cult dates from 716 B.C., but the worship of fire was doubtless much earlier. If the sacred fire died down or was accidentally put out, it was again kindled by using concave mirrors of brass, even as in Peru. The long history of this cult is told by Sir T. Cato Worsfold, who concludes:

"It is significant of the hold which their cult obtained over the religious life of Rome that their functions remained unchanged and their importance increased rather than diminished, in spite of the many political upheavals in the evolution of the Roman people.

"Nothing less than a complete revolution in religious thought, and the advent of a greater Faith, was powerful

[30] *De Civitate Dei*, iii. 28.

THE ORIGIN OF FIRE-WORSHIP

enough to destroy the worship that had defied the chances and changes of a thousand years.

"Through all the phases of Rome's evolution, from the early hamlet to the Eternal City, the sacredness of the family hearth remained the foundation of Roman religious feeling, symbolized by the little Temple of Mother Vesta, the mysterious goddess of whom no statue was ever made." [31]

3. Fire is also found in widespread areas of culture, both primitive and secondary, as *a method of communion with the Divine*. This is generally in one of three forms: either a fire on the hearth to propitiate the household gods, fire on the altar to release the sacrifice, or fire with incense to please or propitiate the gods by its sweet smell. We select only a few examples from each of these methods of using fire in worship.

There was always thought to be special virtue in the perpetuation of the hearth-fire. It was guarded with care, and its extinction was a bad omen. In the hut of the chief of the Thonga tribe in South Africa a perpetual fire burns. "It must be fed with special wood provided by a certain clan. It is taboo to take embers from this fire. The hut and the chief's wife, keeper of the sacred fire, are taboo." [32] Frazer and other students of folk-lore give many similar instances from tribes in Africa, Asia, and America. The idea that fire could be contaminated and that there was "strange

[31] *History of the Vestal Virgins*, pp. 18, 19, 153.

[32] Henri A. Junod, *The Life of a South African Tribe*, vol. i, 1913, p. 364. Many other references are found in the same work.

THE ORIGIN OF FIRE-WORSHIP

fire" occurs in many places. Stolen fire is taboo in Polynesia; in other places fire is contaminated by spitting or even by the pointing of a spear or a sharp instrument. Pure fire is (as we have seen in the case of the Zoroastrians) obtained by a long process. Even the priest who officiates at the fire-worship wears a white cloth over his face lest he contaminate it with his breath. The Hindus have similar burdensome customs to obtain or retain purity of fire. In all this we have a sidelight on the enigmatic statement regarding Nadab and Abihu in Lev. 10: 1-3.

It is obvious that in the history of animal sacrifice and of human sacrifice, fire was the element that transferred the offering from man to the gods and from earth to heaven. Except among the ancient Persians the *altar-fires* were the symbol of sacrificial worship. So true is this that "perhaps the clearest traces of sacrifice among the early Celts are to be found in the case of the Beltane fires of Scotland and Ireland, and of the bonfires in other Celtic countries." [33]

Scientific theories for the origin of sacrifice are mutually contradictory. Tylor and Spencer, Robertson Smith and Jevons, Mauss and Frazer all offer various suggestions but do not agree except that the essential nature of sacrifice is communion with the gods. If we accept the testimony of the Scriptures, the sacrifice offered on the altar was accepted of God by fire. And not only in Israel but among the nations, *the god*

[33] "Encyclopedia of Religion and Ethics," Celtic Sacrifice, vol. xi, p. 10.

THE ORIGIN OF FIRE-WORSHIP

that answered by fire, he is God. When the altar fires die to ashes worship ceases, but the smoke of the altar is the universal symbol of the act of worship.

Not only piacular victims were laid on the altar for the gods, but sweet-smelling incense was burned with fire to propitiate the unseen powers. The earliest routes of land travel, says Sprenger, were the *weihrauchstrasse,* the incense-roads, of Arabia. On Ptolemy's map the whole of southern Asia is marked Libanotopheros Regio, and Pliny termed it Regio Thurifera, "incense country." Frankincense went from here by caravan to Egypt and Babylonia before the dawn of history. Sprenger devotes several pages describing the extent and influence of this trade on antiquity.[84]

If the smoke of sacrifice was pleasing to the gods, the smoke of costly frankincense would be also. It became a symbol of prayer ascending to the gods and its ritual use was common at a very early period in all the ethnic religions. The American Indians had as a substitute the offering of tobacco smoke, while in Polynesia they use aromatic plants, and, among the Malays, benzoin.[85] In every instance it was *burning* that carried the sweet smell to the unseen world of spirits; fire was the agent of transfer from worshiper to the Worshiped. The history of the use of incense in divine worship goes back to the earliest ages and extends to the present. From Egypt, Babylonia, Assyria, Persia,

[84] Zwemer, *Arabia the Cradle of Islam,* p. 18. Sprenger, *Alte Geographie Arabiens,* 1875, pp. 398 ff., 429 ff.
[85] "Encyclopedia of Religion and Ethics," article, Incense.

India, China, Greece, and Rome we have examples of its use and its importance in worship. In ancient Egypt there was a temple official, in 3000 B.C., with the title "Chief of the House of Incense," who presided over incense offerings. In the Creation Story of the Babylonians (1500 B.C.) we are told of the hero who survived the flood:

"I made a libation on the summit of the mountain.
By sevens I set out the vessels.
Under them I heaped up calamus, cedar-wood, and *rig-gir*.
The gods smelt the sweet savor." [86]

In ancient Israel incense was offered morning and evening on the golden altar (Exod. 30: 7, 8) and for making atonement (Lev. 16: 12; Luke 1: 10). When it was unlawfully offered, severe penalties followed (Num. 16: 16-35). The altar for burnt-offering stood in the holy place, that for incense was in the Holy of Holies, while in John's vision there is an altar for incense in heaven itself (Rev. 8: 2; 9: 13). We see in every one of these instances, both among Jews and Gentiles, that the use of incense is a symbol of communion with God. Men drew near to him by fire, who is himself consuming fire.[87]

---

[86] E. G. Cuthbert Atchley, *A History of the Use of Incense in Divine Worship* (London, 1901), p. 17.

[87] "The flame of my life burns low
Under the cluttered days, like a fire of leaves.
But always a little blue sweet-smelling smoke
Goes up to God."
               (*Karl Wilson Baker*)

THE ORIGIN OF FIRE-WORSHIP

4. Finally we have evidence that fire-baptism, the flame of fire, the halo or the disk of light, are all used as symbols of heaven-sent grace or favor. And this not only in Judaism and Christianity, but in such wide and unexpected groups of culture that the only explanation seems to be a primitive sense or intuition that fire and flame are gifts of the gods.

Light is one of the attributes of deity. It is penetrating, intangible, shines afar off, and is not harmful but beneficial. Many fire-gods are also light-gods. Myths regarding the origin of light are rare compared with those regarding the origin of fire. Yet in many of the ethnic religions we have the "feast-of-lights," e.g., the Lupercalia at Rome, the feast of lamps in memory of Isis in Egypt, the Japanese feast of lanterns, and similar occasions in India and China. The perpetual light, as the perpetual fire, finds a place in many religions. The Jewish *Nur-tamid* is as familiar as the altar-lamps in Roman Catholic churches. Both symbolize the presence of God, who is light. Therefore too we find the use of candles in all the great religions of the world. Fire and light have purifying significance. The purification therefore in many cults is done by fire. Walter Hough gives instances among the American Indians and in Burma, Borneo, and Tartary.[38]

Ordeal by fire is a primitive substitute for law. The custom goes back to great antiquity. Men were "tried as by fire" to prove innocence or guilt. The

[38] *Op. cit.*, p. 173.

Greeks also practiced this ordeal. In the Antigone of Sophocles, Creon is assured that all the guards were faithful and ready,

> "Either red-hot bars to take up with our hands
> Or pass through fires, or by the gods to swear
> That neither in the body did we enter
> Nor privy to the wicked action were."

It is only a step from this temporary contact with fire unharmed, to the higher degree of touch with the Divine when fire or flame rests on those who are innocent or saintly enough to be favored of heaven. We refer to the halo or nimbus of glory found in art among many nations.

Moses' face shone after his sojourn on the holy mountain. Stephen's face before his martyrdom was illuminated like that of an angel. The pillar-of-fire was the sign of God's presence in the wilderness and the tongues-of-fire witnessed to the descent of the Spirit at Pentecost. Religious art has adopted this symbolism and it goes back to early Egypt.[39] There we see on the monuments Amen-Ra and Rat with the golden disk on their heads. The disk may be the original of the aureole, the nimbus, horns of light, and the halo, for all these are found in art to represent nearness to God. The aureole takes various forms. Sometimes it circles the head only, and again the whole body. In relief sculpture there is a frame or band in some cases a gilded ring maintained by slight supports. In Bud-

[39] E. A. W. Budge, *Gods of the Egyptians,* vol. i, pp. 328, 330.

dhist art it is very decorative and takes the form of a nimbus or cloud of light. The *vesica piscis* is an aureole of pointed oval shape quite common in Christian art. Again we have flames above the brow or the cruciferous nimbus. Buddha, Brahma, Krishna, and other Indian gods are represented with a nimbus and starlike rays.[40] The nimbus in Christian art appeared first in the fifth century, but it is found much earlier in India and Egypt. Its use has been traced through the Egyptians to the Greeks and Romans. But the supernatural radiance on Moses' face and the "cloven tongues like as of fire" on the heads of the apostles, not to speak of the theophanies of the Old Testament or the Transfiguration and the glory of our Risen Redeemer as he appeared to John on Patmos—all these are not art or symbol but reality. They bring us back to where we began. "Our God is a consuming fire." He dwells in light inaccessible and full of glory. The light of the knowledge of the glory of the transcendent Father is in the face of his Son Jesus Christ. The mystery of fire and light go back to the first day of creation and the human family have carried the tradition of that Genesis to every corner of the globe.[41]

[40] O. M. Dalton, *Late Christian Art*. Charles Coleman, *Hindu Mythology*. London, 1832.

[41] Cf. Edwyn Bevan *Symbolism and Belief*. In the sixth lecture he deals with light as symbol of deity in all parts of the world pp. 125-150.

CHAPTER SEVEN

THE ORIGIN OF MARRIAGE AND PRIMITIVE ETHICS

NOW a casual observer of savage life is apt to imagine it a welter of amatory confusion. Nay, responsible theorists have vied with each other in depicting a primal condition of society when marriage simply was not, and the habits of the barnyard or the rabbit-warren predominated instead. Whether termed crudely promiscuity, or cryptically hetairism, or pedantically agamy, or euphemistically communal marriage, or delicately primitive indifference, the state of affairs thus variously indicated was such as must have caused the student of early man to blush, had any power of television enabled him to look upon it. Fortunately, he has been spared the unseemly sight, and in the meantime is too busy to listen to disreputable stories about forerunners whose historical status is about on a par with that of the fairies. On the other hand, the real savage as we observe him is so far from being a votary of free love that he is rather the victim of an all-too-legal matrimony."

R. R. MARETT,
in FAITH, HOPE, AND CHARITY
IN PRIMITIVE RELIGION, *p. 77*.

CHAPTER SEVEN

THE ORIGIN OF MARRIAGE AND PRIMITIVE ETHICS

A RECENT BOOK DEALING WITH THE HISTORY OF REligion is entitled *The Rainbow Bridge*. The first chapter is about the creed of the cave-man. Primitive man is here portrayed in all his nakedness of soul and body —a religious animal who worships a beast! The sacred beast or totem was regarded as the founder of the clan. "He was Alpha and Omega, the beginning and the end." "The Kangaroo-man lived on the kangaroo and married a Kangaroo woman." "All of our knowledge and philosophy began with the cult of a totem-animal which was the creed of the cave-man." [1]

---

[1] John Story Newberry, *The Rainbow Bridge*, pp. 1-23. We read in the Foreword: "This tale of beasts and man and demi-gods and gods traces the history of paganism from the Stone Age to the Age of Pericles. I have undertaken to analyze the ideas that formed the basis of the religious cults of the cave men, the Sumerians, the Chinese and Japanese, the Hindus, the Egyptians, the Persians, the Hebrews, the Phrygians, and the Greeks, and to coordinate these different racial attempts to exploit the supernatural, thus showing how the beliefs of the savage evolved into the creed of the most enlightened race of ancient times." The same theory controls a book by Frederick Engels on *The Origin of the Family*, "Private Property and the State," pp. 27-35. Translated from the German. 4th edition, Chicago, 1910.

Primitive man, according to this theory, was utterly unable to draw fine distinctions between soul and body or spirit and matter. Fear controlled him. His passions were given free scope. He had no love or faith, only hate and lust. Sexual license controlled by a few taboos was at the basis of family life, if there was a family at all. "The actual course of development," writes Lewis Browne, "out of which were evolved the ideas of sin, conscience, and post-mortem retribution was, to be sure, not so simple. . . . . For centuries man fumbled about to lay hold of these ideas blundering off into the most pathetic errors and beating his way back only with horridest pain . . . . but finally the great task was accomplished and morality preserved." [2]

But whatever the condition of the so-called "caveman," he must have been a social being and had a family. That was prior to all else in the history of progress. Around the family, as Chesterton says, "gather the sanctities that separate men from ants and bees. Decency is the curtain of that tent; liberty is the wall of that city; property is the family farm; and honor is the family flag." [3]

There is no tribe or clan, no speech or language in the wide world, where this ancient trinity of father, mother, and child does not exist. In spite of all the pseudo-scientific gossip about promiscuity, marriage by capture, or the picture of the cave-man beating the

[2] Lewis Browne, *This Believing World*, p. 53. Cf. H. G. Wells, *Outline of History*, ch. i.
[3] G. K. Chesterton, *The Everlasting Man*, p. 44.

MARRIAGE AND PRIMITIVE ETHICS 183

cave-woman with a club, the verdict of science today agrees rather with the statement in Gen. 2: 18-25: "And the man said, This is now bone of my bone and flesh of my flesh, and she shall be called woman, because she was taken out of man. Therefore shall a man leave his father and his mother, and shall cleave unto his wife, and they shall be one flesh."

Biologically, every community must rest on the family, and the first point to be noted, according to the anthropologist Robert H. Lowie, is the bilateral character involved in that concept. The family as a social unit includes *both* parents and in a secondary sense the kindred on both sides. "The question then that concerns us above all others is whether primitive tribes recognize this bilateral principle in their conception of family life."[4] And after a careful discussion, Lowie concludes that in spite of matriarchal and patriarchal variations of custom, in spite of the sexual division of labor, "the bilateral family is none the less an absolutely universal unit of human society."[5] "Neither morphologically nor dynamically can social life be said to have progressed from a stage of savagery to a stage of enlightenment."[6]

Under the influence of the evolutionary hypothesis the trend of anthropology was to assert promiscuity, communal marriage, or polygamy as the earliest form of social organization. This view has been advanced

[4] *Primitive Society*, p. 64.
[5] *Ibid.*, p. 78.
[6] *Ibid.*, p. 440.

by Bachofen, Morgan, and McLennan. It has found support in such distinguished writers as Howitt, Tylor, Spencer, Frazer, and others. But it was combatted by Darwin, Westermarck, Lang, Grosse, Crawley, and most recently by Brunislaw Malinowski, Professor of Anthropology in the University of London.[7] The subject is of considerable importance, not only biologically, but also in the realm of ethics.

"The suppositions on which the sex reformers rely," says Sidney Dark, "have been shown by the defenders of Christianity to be false. The appeal which was once confidently made to the promiscuity practiced by the earliest groups of mankind, and the elaborate description of development through matriarchy have had to be abandoned. The available evidence points always to the primary importance of marriage and family in primitive societies. The appeal again to biology to support the modern theory that sexual love has no necessary connection with the propagation of the species has not been borne out by the facts."[8]

Westmarck, in his first chapter on the origin of human marriage, refers to the relation of the sexes among animals:

"Most birds, with the exception of those belonging to the Gallinaceous family, when pairing, do so once for all till either one or the other dies. And Dr. Brehm is so filled with admiration for their exemplary family life that

[7] See his article on "Marriage" in the Encyclopedia Britannica, Fourteenth Edition, vol. xiv, pp. 940-950.

[8] Sidney Dark, *Orthodoxy Sees It Through*, p. 56.

MARRIAGE AND PRIMITIVE ETHICS 185

he enthusiastically declares that 'real genuine marriage can only be found among birds.'"

This is not the case among mammals. But there are here important exceptions. He gives as instances whales, seals, gazelles, antelope, reindeer, squirrels, moles, etc. Among all these animals the sexes remain together, by pairs, even after the birth of the young, the male being the protector of the family. What among lower mammals is an exception is among the quadrumana a rule.[9]

After describing the various forms of human marriage, polyandry, polygyny, and polygamy, and explaining the motives that led to these abnormal conditions, Malinowski states:

"Monogamy is not only the most important form of marriage, not only that which predominates in most communities, and which occurs, statistically speaking, in an overwhelming majority of instances, but it is also the pattern and prototype of marriage.

"Both polyandry and polygyny are compound marriages, consisting of several unions combined into a larger system, but each of them constituted into a pattern of a monogamous marriage. As a rule polygamous cohabitation is a successive monogamy and not joint domesticity; children and property are divided, and in every other respect the contracts are entered individually between two partners at a time. . . . .

"Monogamy as pattern and prototype of human marriage, on the other hand, is universal. The whole institution, in the sexual, parental, economic, legal, and religious

[9] *The History of Human Marriage*, pp. 11-15.

aspects, is founded on the fact that the real function of marriage—sexual union, production and care of children, and the co-operation which it implies—requires essentially two people, and two people only, and that in the overwhelming majority of cases two people only are united in order to fulfil these facts.

"Conjugation necessarily takes place only between two organisms; children are produced by two parents only, and always socially regarded as the offspring of one couple; the economics of the household are never conducted group-wise; the legal contract is never entered upon jointly; the religious sanction is given only to the union of two. A form of marriage based on communism in sex, joint parenthood, domesticity, group-contract, and a promiscuous sacrament has never been described. Monogamy is, has been, and will remain the only true type of marriage. To place polygyny and polyandry as 'forms of marriage, co-ordinate with monogamy is erroneous. To speak about 'group-marriage' as another variety shows a complete lack of understanding as to the nature of marriage."

The mass of evidence on which these conclusions are based is found in Malinowski's own book, *Sex and Repression in Savage Society*, but more especially in Westermarck's great work, *The History of Human Marriage*, in three volumes.[10] Dr. Edward Westermarck was lecturer on Sociology at the University of Finland, Helsingfors, and his authority is unquestioned. We therefore make no apology to quote once more from this standard work:

[10] Our references and quotations are from the abridged one-volume edition by Macmillan & Co., New York, 1891. He gives a list of over seven hundred authorities in his thirty pages of bibliography.

MARRIAGE AND PRIMITIVE ETHICS

"In all probability there has been no stage of human development when marriage has not existed and thus the father has always been as a rule the protector of the family." [11]

After examining the so-called evidence for an early stage of promiscuity, according to Bachofen, Lubbock, and others, he quotes Mr. Man regarding the Andamanese that "they are strictly monogamous, that divorce is unknown, and conjugal fidelity till death not the exception but the rule." [12] In the case of some African tribes Westermarck admits that sexual relations seem to be promiscuous.

"On the other hand, among the lowest races on earth, as the Veddahs, Fuegians, and Australians, the relations of the sexes are of a much more definite character. The Veddahs are a truly monogamous people, and have a saying that 'death alone separates husband and wife.'" [13]

And afterward Westermarck concludes:

"Having now examined all the groups of social phenomena adduced as evidence for the hypothesis of promiscuity, we have found that, in point of fact, there is no evidence. Not one of the customs alleged as relics of an ancient state of indiscriminate cohabitation of the sexes, or 'communal marriage,' presupposes the former existence of that state. The numerous facts put forward in support of the hypothesis do not entitle us to assume that promiscuity has ever been the prevailing form of sexual relations among a single people, far less that it has constituted a general stage in the social development of man, and, least

---

[11] Westermarck, *History of Human Marriage*, p. 50.
[12] *Ibid.*, p. 57.
[13] *Ibid.*, p. 60.

of all, that such a stage formed the starting point of human history."[14]

Not only has the hypothesis of promiscuity no basis in fact. Westermarck goes on to demonstrate that it is "opposed to all the correct ideas we are able to form with regard to the early condition of man." Jealousy and the rights of property demanded chastity on the part of women among the Chippewas, the Aztecs, in Samoa, and in New Guinea.[15] The idea that a woman belongs exclusively to one man is deep-rooted everywhere and the deceased husband may torment a wife after death if she proves unfaithful.[16]

"But there is not a shred of genuine evidence for the notion that promiscuity ever formed a general stage in the social history of mankind. The hypothesis of promiscuity, instead of belonging, as Professor Giraud-Teulon thinks, to the class of hypotheses which are scientifically permissible, has no real foundation, and is essentially unscientific."[17]

We will conclude with one more quotation from Westermarck:

"Summing up the results reached in this chapter, we may safely say that, although polygyny occurs among most existing peoples, and polyandry among some, monogamy is by far the most common form of human marriage. It was so also among the ancient peoples of whom we have any direct knowledge. Monogamy is the form which is generally recognized as legal and permitted. The great

[14] Westmarck, *op. cit.*, p. 113.
[15] *Ibid.*, p. 123.
[16] *Ibid.*, p. 130.
[17] *Ibid.*, p. 133.

majority of peoples are, as a rule, monogamous, and the other forms of marriage are usually modified in a monogamous direction."[18]

It would be possible to add here the testimony of a score of other witnesses, in addition to Westermarck, whose names are well-known in anthropology.[19] They all agree that the family is the central pillar of all social life among primitives; that love for mother and for wife is not nominal but real; and that, generally speaking, polyandry where known is the product, not of a primitive state, but of a perverted civilization.[20] Further it is generally agreed that exogamy (or marriage outside of the clan) is almost universal and that no crime is considered so great as that of incest.

A new theory on totemism is put forward in *Man* (September, 1931), by C. Bullock, who draws his conclusions from observations made among the Mashona Tribes. Totemism there stands in close relation to exogamy, and certain taboos regulating the use of

[18] Westermarck, *op. cit.*, p. 459.

[19] Dr. J. D. Unwin, late Fellow Commoner Research Student, Peterhouse, Cambridge, has conducted a detailed inquiry into the relation between sexual opportunity and cultural condition among uncivilized and civilized peoples. The bulk of his book, *Sex and Culture* (Oxford, 1934), is devoted to the evidence provided by anthropologists and the customs of eighty uncivilized peoples have been examined. Among such peoples Dr. Unwin distinguishes three main types of cultural pattern—the deistic which is characterized by the building of temples, the manistic characterized by the paying of post-funeral attention to the dead, and the zoistic, in which the people did neither of these things. On the basis of his careful researches Dr. Unwin is able to show that all deistic communities insist on pre-nuptial chastity, all manistic communities insist on an irregular or occasional continence, while all zoistic communities permit pre-nuptial freedom.

[20] Le Roy, *The Religion of Primitives*, pp. 62-70.

totem words between the sexes, as well as the meaning of these totem words, indicate that sexual thought, especially the avoidance of incest, is the inherent attribute of totemism. This fact leads Mr. Bullock to propound the following theory: "The social group is not exogamous because totemic, but vice versa. Totemism is a consequence of exogamy; it is the artificial concept which has followed the natural thought."

Totemism is a device employed by primitive man to unite, distinguish, and strengthen the family tie through a magical pact. Consanguineous unions are nearly everywhere taboo.[21] "Incest is the sin of sins and is therefore tolerated only among the most exceptional conditions. . . . . Incest and the shedding of tribal blood together with witchcraft—these alone are the three deadly sins," that cannot be forgiven among primitives.[22]

One of the most exhaustive studies on primitive marriage is that by E. Crawley, who concludes: "It may be confidently assumed that individual marriage has been, so far as we can trace it back, the regular type of union of man and woman. The promiscuity theory really belongs to the mythological stage of human intelligence . . . . these myths are interesting but of no scientific value."[23]

[21] Le Roy, *op. cit.*, pp. 70, 87.

[22] R. R. Marett, *Faith, Hope, and Charity in Primitive Religions*, pp. 91, 92. New York, 1932.

[23] *The Mystic Rose:* A Study of Primitive Marriage, p. 483.

MARRIAGE AND PRIMITIVE ETHICS 191

Malinowski, in referring to this monograph, says:

"Another important result of Mr. Crawley's work is the establishment of the principle that marriage rites, being the breaking of a dangerous taboo, are an essential part of marriage, and therefore their study is essential for the understanding of this institution. The rites, being exclusively intended to break the taboo between two individuals and not between two groups, lead to individual marriage and family, and not to 'group marriage' and 'group family.'

"To corroborate my supposition that marriage ceremonies are much more frequent in Australia than stated by the authorities I may quote Mr. Crawley's view. He says that 'as to those (peoples) who are said to possess no marriage ceremony, it will generally be found that there is some act performed which is too slight or too practical to be marked by an observer as a "ceremony," but which when analyzed turns out to be a real marriage rite.' " [24]

According to Grosse, not only is there no evidence of group-marriage among Australian aborigines, but the husband is sole proprietor.[25]

Seligmann, in his monograph on the *Veddas,* one of the most primitive tribes, living in the mountains of Ceylon, says:

"The Veddas are strictly monogamous, and we were able to confirm Bailey's observations as regards their marital fidelity. 'Their constancy to their wives is a very remarkable trait in their character in a country where conjugal fidelity is certainly not classed as the highest of

[24] *Family Life among the Australian Aborigines,* pp. 305, 306.
[25] Helen Bosanquet, *The Family,* p. 29. For detailed evidence on the priority of monogamy among primitives cf. Schmidt, *Ursprung der Gottesidee,* vol. i, pp. 224-235.

domestic virtues. Infidelity, whether in the husband or the wife, appears to be unknown, and I was very careful in my inquiries on this subject. Had it existed, the neighboring Sinhalese would have had no hesitation in accusing them of it, but I could not obtain a trace of it.' " [26]

In regard to the head-hunters of Borneo, we have the testimony of Carl Lumholtz that monogamy is the general practice, only the chief being allowed to have five or more wives, and even this was at the displeasure of his immediate family.[27] The same is true of the Andamanese, whose social organization, marriage rites, and duties are all based on the monogamous ideal. "Conjugal fidelity till death is not the exception but the rule." [28]

Now if marriage according to the evolutionary theory "was transmitted to man from some distant apelike ancestor" it is impossible to account for such high ideals among Primitives, for "we may safely affirm," said Alfred Russell Wallace, "that the better specimens of savages are much superior to the lower examples of civilized peoples." [29] The temporary American citizens of Reno might learn from the fidelity of some savage tribes or even from the *quadrumana* what God intended the family to be, because the orang-utan, for example,

"live in families—the male, female, and a young one. On occasion I found a family in which there were two young ones, one of them much larger than the other, and

[26] *The Veddas*, pp. 87, 88, Cambridge, 1911.

[27] *Through Central Borneo*, vol. i, p. 199.

[28] A. R. Brown, *The Andaman Islanders*, p. 70.

[29] Quoted as motto text to his *Travels in Central Borneo* by Carl Lumholtz, vol. i, p. vi.

MARRIAGE AND PRIMITIVE ETHICS 193

I took this as a proof that the family tie had existed for at least two seasons. They build commodious nests in the trees which form their feeding-ground, and, so far as I could observe, the nests, which are well lined with dry leaves, are only occupied by the female and young, the male passing the night in the fork of the same or another tree in the vicinity." [30]

We turn from the primitive marriage to the origin of the moral idea. Man universally is possessed of a faculty which we may call conscience. Earlier writers of the evolutionary school asserted that in many savage races the moral sense was utterly lacking. A recent writer on Egyptology calls his book *The Dawn of Conscience*. He places the first moral judgment about the year 3500 B.C. Until then, he infers, the words for right and wrong are not in the Egyptian vocabulary.[31] Over against this we may place the judgment of an earlier writer, Quatrefages, who affirms:

"Confining ourselves rigorously to the region of facts, and carefully avoiding the territory of philosophy and theology, we may state without hesitation that there is no human society, or even association, in which the idea of good and evil is not represented by certain acts regarded by the members of that society or association as morally good and morally bad. Even among robbers and pirates theft is regarded as a misdeed, sometimes as a crime, and severely punished, while treachery is branded with infamy. The facts noticed by Wallace among the Karubars and Santals show how the consciousness of moral good and

[30] William I. Thomas, *Source Book for Social Origins*, p. 450.
[31] J. H. Breasted, *The Dawn of Conscience*.

truth is anterior to experience and independent of questions of utility."[32]

Not only do all men recognize moral distinctions as shown by the law of taboos and the horror of incest, but they recognize moral obligations. Modern social psychologists teach that moral impulses originated out of influences operating in family relationships. In other words, the family tie is the basis of tribal morals. According to the Bible, the Dawn of Conscience came with the fall of man and the tragedy of sin. And if we accept this there is no more vivid and accurate picture of such a dawn which "came up like thunder," than in the third chapter of Genesis. Yet there is no chapter in the Bible the interpretation of which has been more affected by prejudgments, scientific or philosophical, than this one. It is remarkable, however, that the latest anthropological studies seem to fit, as a key to the lock, the great concepts of that chapter.

R. R. Marett, in his recent book *Faith, Hope, and Charity in Primitive Religion*, challenges attention by its very title. After speaking of the universality of religion and of its emotional content, he goes on to say:

"There are unhelpful, not to say positively harmful, propensities almost or quite as universal as the religious tendency; and it would be paradoxical to argue that we are any the better for having to stagger along under this pilgrim's burden, *this load of original sin*."[33] (The italics are not Marett's.)

[32] *The Human Species*, p. 459.
[33] *Faith, Hope, and Charity in Primitive Religion*, p. 5.

Religion is the central fact of savage society, he says, but we make a mistake if we look only on the surface of primitive cult and ritual.

"One might as well try to extract literature from a glossary as to read a religious significance into the interminable catalogue of savage gods and godlings which the less enlightened of our field-workers so laboriously compile. These have for the most part little more than what might be called incantation-value." [84]

What really matters is the religion of the heart which even in the savage includes faith, hope, and love. "Born in the mud like the other beasts, man alone refuses to be a stick-in-the-mud"; he aspires to reach higher, and, millenniums before Walter Lippman, he writes his own Preface to Morals!

This includes first of all loyalty to the kin-group; for kinly feeling is kindly feeling in the making. The typical savage regards his elders, alive or dead, as the embodiments of wisdom and power. "It has been true of man," says Marett, "since the times of the Ice Age that the grave itself cannot make an end of family affection." [85] The origin of exogamy is obscure to science—not to those who read the third chapter of Genesis. Westermarck believes that it is "an instinct against inbreeding." But as it meets us in history it is a full-fledged institution with moral sanctions and penalties. Another primary idea is the sacredness of

[84] *Op. cit.*, p. 9.
[85] Article on Rudimentary Ethics in "Encyclopedia of Religion and Ethics," p. 432.

motherhood and of woman's blood. Hence the numberless taboos in this regard.[36] And we are told that these ceremonial customs, starting as taboo in ceremonial aversion, "become almost universally moralized as purity of heart . . . . that develops into the confession of sins." [37]

Where we have in all, or most, of these primitive tribes such elementary moral concepts, together (as we shall see later) with a firm belief in life after death, it becomes impossible to hold to the evolutionary origin of the moral imperative. Not Evolution but Revelation lies back of Faith, Hope, and Charity in primitive religion. Not Evolution but only a primitive Revelation can account for the Dawn of Conscience and for belief in a Day of Doom. How has the non-moral "tangle-of-apes" been transmitted into moral man? Who has taught these savages knowledge above the beasts of the field?

The birth of conscience and the moral idea has been explained on purely naturalistic grounds in three ways: by Utilitarian philosophy, by Evolutionary Hedonism, and by so-called Emergent Evolution. Bentham, Hume, and Mill are advocates of the first theory. They say man became moral because certain actions were conducive of pleasure or saved from pain. Self-interest produced ethics.

The Evolutionary theorists of Hedonism had as their

[36] "Encyclopedia of Religion and Ethics," Article, Rudimentary Ethics, p. 431.
[37] *Ibid.*, p. 435.

protagonist Herbert Spencer—and for them happiness was the dictator of conduct. Both theories fail to show the origin of morals. As Dr. Harold C. Morton, dealing with these three theories in a very thoughful paper, remarks:

"Evolution does not alter the essentials of the problem. It adds the element of almost limitless time. It claims that associations have been fixed in the brain by inheritance through long generations. The illusion of the independence of the Moral Imperative is made easier, but it is an illusion still. No cause has been shown which could by any possibility transform a counsel of prudence concerning the way to find pleasure and avoid pain into the sublime Imperative of the Spirit which bids us do the right for its own sake, in scorn of consequence of any sort." [88]

And in regard to the theory of Emergent Evolution, advocated by C. Lloyd Morgan and W. Macdougall, he writes:

"Thus Emergent Evolution offers no *explanation* of the Moral Imperative, nor of any other 'emergent qualities.' It simply asks us to accept, without any 'power that works changes,' the assumption that these qualities did emerge, and in an order which fits in with evolutionary speculation. All this we are to accept with 'natural piety'! Surely it is not for us to accept with natural piety, but to reject with supernatural energy, a philosophy which gets rid of both God and Cause in order to effect its purpose. Emergent Evolution is an admission of the failure to show cause for the origin of the Moral Imperative; and still the great

[88] "The Supposed Evolutionary Origin of the Moral Imperative" in the *Journal of the Victoria Institute,* London, vol. lxv, p. 156.

Imperative of our Moral Life sounds forth, unexplained and unexplainable save on this one foundation: 'And God said, Let us make man in our image, after our likeness.' "[39]

We repeat, that the only adequate explanation for the presence of the moral idea and of moral ideals in primitive religions is primitive revelation. "For when the Gentiles who have not the law do by nature the things contained in the law, these, having not the law, are a law unto themselves: which show the work of the law written in their hearts, their conscience also bearing witness, and their thoughts the meanwhile accusing or else excusing one another" (Rom. 2: 14, 15). As a matter of fact, human ethics have always been based rightly or wrongly on religious sanctions. Religion precedes morality. This is clear because the breaking of taboo or witchcraft or murder are regarded not merely as wrongs done against a man's neighbor, but against the God or the gods of the community.[40] The conception of a High-god or Sky-god who knows all and sees all, of a God who is immortal and benevolent, must also, surely, be related to primitive ethics. Paul, in his preaching on Mars' Hill to cultured pagans, and in his missionary journeys among more or less primitive races, appealed to the natural conscience (Acts 14: 15-17). "Because that which may be known of God is manifest in them for God hath shewed it unto them. For the invisible things of him from the creation of the

[39] *Op. cit.*, p. 164.
[40] Jevons, *Introduction to Comparative Religion*, p. 221.

MARRIAGE AND PRIMITIVE ETHICS 199

world are clearly seen, being understood by the things which are made even his eternal power and Godhead, so that they are without excuse" (Rom. 1: 19, 20).

The Utilitarian and Emergent evolutionary theories of conscience fail entirely to account for the fact that even among savage races and the most primitive cultures we can see men and women act contrary to self-interest and inclination and even suffer torture and death for what they think is the judgment of their conscience.

Du Chaillu relates of the Aponos near the Equator in Africa that they were an honest people and stole nothing from him, while some always took his part when a dispute arose against him.[41] Livingstone gives many instances of kindness and unselfishness in his Journals. The crowning example, however, is that after his death his two faithful Negro servants carried his body (after they had buried his heart under a tree) with his papers and all his valuables to Zanzibar. They dried the body in the sun, wrapped it in calico, inclosed it in a bark cylinder, sewed a piece of sail-cloth around it, and then set out on their difficult journey. It was nine months' toil on their part without looking for reward. They ran the risk of hostile tribes and wild beasts, but when they met a white party who urged them to bury the body, they refused and persevered! What courage and devotion, what noble loyalty was here! When one stands with bared head in Westmin-

[41] Clark, *Ten Great Religions*, vol. ii, p. 298.

ster Abbey over the grave of Livingstone one cannot forget the first words of the inscription:

> *"Brought by faithful hands over land and sea*
> *Here rests David Livingstone"* ....

It is a tribute to the nobility of the Bantu race and the Negro conscience.

Or take, as a common example, mother-love among all primitive races.

"It is no sacrifice of the mother to suckle her child. Nay, it is the nearest thing to communion on God's earth, and may therefore stand as the perfect symbol of peaceful and bountiful love, as it might be not only in the Communion of Saints, but likewise among us poor human beings. Charity is no late message sent down to civilized folk from heaven. It is something that whispers in the very life-blood of the race; as if it were the tender voice of the Earth-mother bidding us remember that we are all her children." [42]

The words recorded in the book of Acts regarding Paul's experience with the natives of Melita are repeated again and again in missionary annals: "The barbarians showed us no little kindness: for they kindled a fire and received us every one because of the present rain and because of the cold." Who has not been astonished by such hospitality?

With conscience and kindness goes the idea of justice, for we read, regarding the same barbarians, that when they noticed the viper hanging from Paul's hand they

[42] These are the eloquent closing words in Marett's book *Faith, Hope, and Charity in Primitive Religion*, pp. 235, 236.

said among themselves, "No doubt this man is a murderer whom, though he hath escaped the sea, yet justice (vengeance) suffereth not to live."

We do not desire to give a one-sided picture of the virtues of Primitives. Their faults, offenses, crimes, and cruelties are evidence of sin and of age-long degeneration. Slothful, jealous, proud, given to anger, avarice, lust, and lying, their conduct is often shocking to the traveler. As Le Roy says:

"Sometimes a lack of moral sense is met with that quite disconcerts us: it may be a calm and ferocious egoism, or deep conceit, perfect treachery, cool and deliberate cruelty, or a shameless want of pity for the weak, the sick, the useless, the abandoned.

"And yet, withal, what good dispositions we find, what easy and ever ready hospitality, what fidelity to their word, what attachment, generosity, disinterestedness, endurance, courage!

"By their reserve and modesty these savages frequently give civilized man wonderful surprises. Vices against nature are everywhere rare and seem even to be unknown in many places." [43]

R. E. Dennett even cites a series of commandments that constitute the ethical code of the Bavili tribe of Loango in Africa:

"The Bavili have a very distinct idea of the moral and natural law, and classify their sins into five distinct sections of the one great class of laws called Xina, or things forbidden.

[43] *The Religion of the Primitives*, p. 160.

"The first section is called Xina Xivanga Nzambi, or that which is contrary to God the Creator.

"The second refers to the magic-mirror—resembling photography—into which only the *Nganga Nzambi* (the 'seeing of God') may look to discover therein the successor of the chief of Loango, made, they say, after the image of God.

"The third we find in the way the mothers correct their children when they talk foolishly of God.

"The fourth prescribes the observance of each fourth day. On this day 'the prince or father may have no connection with his wife, he may not go outside of his town, he may not hold a palaver. The doctor of Nganga Bilongo may not bleed his patient. The women may not work in the fields.

"The fifth comprises all those ceremonies and things forbidden concerning maternity." [44]

All of such commandments have the sanction of the High-god who is referred to in them. The fact that the primitive High-god has a moral character is very significant. Schmidt, in his summary of the attributes of the High-god, says:

"As regards morality, the primitive Supreme Being is without exception unalterably righteous; his only connection with anything morally bad is to abhor and punish it. The true source of this deeply moral character of the Supreme Being is the fact that he is the first and highest, the giver of the moral law, and consequently its origin; a point on which we shall have more to say later. For the very reason that all evil is kept far from the Supreme Being, those peoples which lay especially great emphasis

[44] Dennett, *At the Back of the Black Man's Mind*, pp. 50-52.

on his moral character oppose to him another being who is the representative of evil, who meets all his endeavors for good with protests and hindrances. We cannot properly call this dualism, for the good Supreme Being is represented as far the stronger and more important; but the origin and continuance of the evil being is often shrouded in a dim twilight which our present knowledge does not allow us to brighten. This is the state of the case among Arctic primitives, the Samoyeds and the Ainu, and the most part of the primitive peoples of North America, for instance the North Central Californians, the tribes of the Northwest and both the Western and Eastern Algonquin." [45]

The Supreme Being among all Pygmy peoples and also among the Samoyeds, Ainu, North Central Californians, Algonquin, Tierra del Fuegans, and Southeast Australians is held to be the author of the moral code. "In general," says Schmidt, "the morality of these primitive races is by no means low; a clear proof that they really follow the ethical commands and prohibitions of their Supreme Being." [46] That is, the conscience or the moral sense is, in their own judgment, closely related to God the Creator—the Sky-god, the One who knows and sees all. How much nearer this primitive faith is to the Scriptures than the vague ethical theories of humanistic liberalism. What would these simple aborigines make of a philosophy that says, "Civilization lies somewhere beyond conscience"?

A recent book by one of this school of thought main-

[45] W. Schmidt, *The Origin and Growth of Religion*, p. 271.
[46] *Ibid.*, p. 274. On this subject compare also Schmidt's *Ursprung der Gottesidee*, vol. vi, pp. 410-439.

tains that conscience cannot be considered the voice of God in the soul, for we can neither prove that God is, or that he is good; nor can conscience be trusted by reason of its own logical authority; nor because of any social sanction approved by society. The only valid reasons for respecting conscience, we are told, are "the aesthetic satisfaction arising from contemplation of our duty tensions and the fact that through conscience alone can its host reach unified selfhood." In a final chapter the Chicago philosopher deduces the principle "that health, individual and social, demands the substitution of understanding of conscience for conscience itself." [47]

After reading such an attempt at sublimating the great moral imperatives by yielding tribute to Freudian behaviorism and Marxist ideology, one turns with relief to the law of God written on tables of stone and on the tables of the human heart. At the Back of the Black Man's Mind, to use Dennett's striking phrase, we find moral ideas that are strangely similar to the Ten Commandments—and not beyond Conscience nor apart from God!

Our conclusion, then, is that we need no longer cross a "Rainbow Bridge" to find a cave-man who by evolutionary processes becomes *homo sapiens;* but that on the threshold of human history and in the earliest cultures he greets us made in the image of God, conscious of his Creator, aware of moral impulses and moral

[47] T. V. Smith, *Beyond Conscience* (New York, 1934), pp. 57, 59, 65, 200, etc.

failure, with the law of God written on his heart and the love of God reflected, although feebly, in a primitive family life, which by all evidence was monogamous. The origin of the family and of conscience is not due to evolution but to a primitive revelation, subjective or objective.

One cannot read the mass of evidence in recent books on ethnology without finding again and again corroboration of the truth of Revelation: "God created man in his own image, male and female created he them." God breathed into his nostrils the breath of Divine life. He made man a little lower than the angels and crowned him with glory and honor. He is our Father, and although we are clay he is our Potter and we are all the work of his hands. Man is the image and glory of God even after the fall, as Paul asserts. God made of one blood all the nations of men. He fashioneth their hearts alike. Have we not all one Father? Hath not one God created us? From the place of his habitation he looketh upon all the inhabitants of the earth. God made man upright, but they have sought out many inventions.[48]

[48] Gen. 1: 27; Ps. 8: 5; Isa. 64: 8; I Cor. 11: 7; Acts 17: 26; Ps. 33: 15; Mal. 2: 10; Ps. 33: 14; Eccles. 7: 29.

CHAPTER EIGHT

THE ORIGIN OF BELIEF IN IMMORTALITY

THUS, then, so far as force of will could do it, Neanderthal man, to whom we grudge the name of *Homo sapiens,* achieved a future life. There can be no question, I think, that the experts are right in attributing to him deliberate burials with due provision for a hereafter. It is even noticeable that funeral custom is already beyond its earliest stage. At La Chapelle-aux-Saints, for instance, not only is the grave neatly dug and food laid by conveniently, but a cave too small for habitation has evidently been selected for a purely sepulchral purpose. If there was a time when the dead man was simply left lying by himself within his own cave-home, or when, perhaps, the dying man was prematurely abandoned, we are well past it."

R. R. MARETT,
FAITH, HOPE AND CHARITY
IN PRIMITIVE RELIGION, *p. 34.*

"Also He hath set eternity in their heart, yet so that man cannot find out the work that God hath done from the beginning even to the end."

ECCLES. 3:11 (Revised Version).

CHAPTER EIGHT

THE ORIGIN OF BELIEF IN IMMORTALITY

PERHAPS THE MOST REMARKABLE FACT IN THE Comparative History of Religion is the universal belief of mankind in a future state of existence after death. Without that faith man sinks to the level of the brute. In Dostoievski's novel, *The Brothers Karamazov*, Ivan says: "If you were to destroy in mankind the belief in immortality, not only love, but every living force containing the life of the world would at once be dried up. Moreover, nothing then would be immoral. Everything would be lawful, including cannibalism. There is no virtue if there is no immortality."

Belief in a future destiny is one of the strongest moral sanctions, and it is this conviction above all else that gives dignity to human nature and action. It gives a meaning and purpose to life, even among savages of the lower cultures; as Charlevoix, a Jesuit missionary, said, "The belief best established among Aboriginal Americans is that of the immortality of the soul."

Men have had this belief everywhere and in all ages. Whatever its origin, we find it among the ancient Egyptians and ancient Hindus; among the Eskimo of the far North and among the tribes of Tierra del Fuego on the extreme South. It cannot therefore be the result of contact with superior cultures or be due to a process of reasoning. It seems to be innate or instinctive. None of the great religions teach that death ends all, and no primitive tribe believes it. Even the Buddhist does not understand Nirvana to be annihilation, but a state or an absorption of the soul into peace and tranquillity. Tennyson is right when he sings:

> "Whatever crazy sorrow saith,
> No life that breathes with human breath
> Hath ever truly longed for death.
> 'Tis life of which our nerves are scant,
> 'Tis life, not death, for which we pant,
> More life and fuller that we want."

Men believe in the immortality of the soul because of the intrinsic incompleteness of the present life. Death closes the door, but we believe it leads to another room because we see that character grows even after the faculties begin to decline.

And among all races there have been those who believed in life eternal because of the imperative clamor of the affections. Not only in Christian lands, but among all races, love is stronger than death. Think of the burial rites of the animist in the deep forests of Africa or in the isles of the South Seas. In ancient Greece or to men like Homer, Cicero, and Plato, there was no question of man's immortality—they believed it. The religion of ancient Egypt proclaims it in tombs and the witness of monuments. What is the Book of the Dead or Tutankhamen's tomb and treasure-house save an abiding witness that these ancients lived for eternity? It is one unbroken testimony from Mexico, Rome, Greece, India, and Africa.

James Freeman Clarke, in writing on the idea of a future life among all races, tells how the ancient tombs of the Etruscans bear inscriptions that whisper faith in immortality:

"One says, 'While we depart to nought, our essence rises'; another, 'We rise like a bird'; another, 'We ascend to our ancestors'; another, 'The soul rises like fire.' They have pictures of the soul seated on a horse, and with a traveling-bag in its hand."[1]

Or take a modern instance. Writing on "Jainism" in the *Review of Nations* (January, 1927), a Hindu, Champat Rai Jain, says:

"Happiness is not possible for him who has constantly the fear of death gnawing at his heart. In short, we want immortality, all-embracing knowledge, and uninterrupted bliss, and will not be satisfied with anything less. Now, *Jainism* discovers that the soul is by its very nature a simple substance as distinguished from a compound thing, endowed with the capacity for infinite all-embracing knowledge, and blissful. The space at my disposal will not admit of my enlarging on any of these essential potentialities of the soul substance, or to undertake their proof. But very strict logical proof is available to prove the *Jaina* claim in this respect. Modern experimental psychology is generally coming round to the view that the soul is a simple

[1] *Ten Great Religions*, vol. ii, p. 326.

substance, and, as such, deathless and immortal. The significance of the simple nature of the soul is that it is incapable of disintegration or of being destroyed, because what is not made up of parts cannot be pulled to pieces in any way. The soul, then, is immortal in its own nature."

So unquestioned and universal is this belief in the immortality of the soul that Sir James Frazer, the great authority on folk-lore and early religious beliefs, requires three volumes to tell of the belief in immortality among primitives.[2] The first volume deals with these beliefs as found among the aborigines of Australia, the Torres Straits, New Guinea, and Melanesia; the second with the races of Polynesia; and the third with the scattered tribes of Micronesia and Indonesia.

Is it not astonishing that some liberal theologians and the Graf-Welhausen school of Bible critics do not find the idea of immortality in the Old Testament? They even state that Moses only knew Jahveh as a tribal god of Sinai. We would ask with Andrew Lang:

"Have critics and manual-makers no knowledge of the science of comparative religion? Are they unaware that peoples infinitely more backward than Israel was at the date supposed, have already moral Supreme Beings acknowledged over vast tracts of territory? Have they a tittle of positive evidence that early Israel was benighted beyond the darkness of Bushmen, Andamanese, Pawnees, Blackfeet, Hurons, Indians of British Guiana, Dinkas, Negroes, and so forth? Unless Israel had this rare ill-luck

[2] James George Frazer, *The Belief in Immortality and the Worship of the Dead*. 3 vol. London, 1922.

ORIGIN OF BELIEF IN IMMORTALITY

(which Israel denies) of course Israel must have had a secular tradition, however dim, of a Supreme Being." [3]

If Israel knew the Supreme God, who can imagine that before or after their sojourn in Egypt *they* were ignorant of the immortality of the soul? The argument from silence in the Pentateuch or the historic books is not conclusive. For example, nothing was more commonplace in the daily life of the Israelites than the date-fruit and the domestic cat. Pictured on the Egyptian monuments and hieroglyphs, both worshiped and embalmed, there is yet no mention of either the date or the cat in the whole Old Testament! So common were they that they escaped mention. May not the belief in survival after death have been a commonplace of the belief of the patriarchs and of Israel? At any rate we have the great passage in Job as an exception that proves the rule, not to speak of references in the Psalms and the Prophets. Dr. James Orr denies emphatically that the Old Testament has no doctrine of immortality. The Hebrews, like every other ancient people, believed that the soul survived the body.

"It is said we have no doctrine of Immortality in the Old Testament. But I reply, we *have* immortality at the very commencement—for man, as he came from the hands of his Creator, was made for immortal life. Man in Eden was immortal. He was intended to live, not to die. Then came sin, and with it death. Adam called his son Seth, and Seth called his son Enoch, which means 'frail, mortal man.' Seth himself died, his son died, his son's son died.

[3] Andrew Lang, *The Making of Religion*, p. 312.

and so the line of death goes on. Then comes an interruption, the intervention, as it were, of a higher law, a new inbreaking of immortality into a line of death. 'Enoch walked with God, and he was not; for God took him.' Enoch did not die. Every other life in that record ends with the statement, 'and he died'; but Enoch's is given as an exception. He did not die, but God 'took' him, i.e., without death." [4]

And then he sums up the evidence from other parts of the Old Testament, not for life after death only, but *for a whole immortality of body and soul and spirit*—namely, the hope of a resurrection, such as the Pharisees held at the time of Christ.

What is even more astonishing than the denial of the doctrine of immortality in the Old Testament is that some Liberals of the humanistic type express no desire for personal immortality or for a life after death. A professor at Harvard University in a brilliant lecture given this year on Indian conceptions of immortality says: "So far as I can discover from observation on myself, the concept of immortality plays little part in my own thought and has had no appreciable influence on the formation of my character or on my conduct. It is hard for me to understand those to whom it is an obsession." [5]

But, as we have noted already, the idea of a future life *is* an obsession with the vast majority of mankind and has been since the earliest ages. The materialistic conception of the universe finds no place among Primi-

[4] Orr, *The Christian View of God and the World*, pp. 200-211.
[5] *The Ingersoll Lecture*, p. 3. Cambridge, Mass., 1934.

tives. Their whole thought-life is molded by animism, i.e., the belief in soul-stuff or *mana* not only in man but in animals and what we call inanimate nature. The body dies; the soul lives on.

The oldest records of the race and the oldest monuments witness to a life beyond the grave. Professor W. E. Hocking thus comments on Bertrand Russell's view that *"When the brain ceases to function the mind ceases to exist; the notion of a separable soul is an illusion"*:

"Certainly these are sane conclusions, favored by every visible appearance; indeed, they are so sane and obvious as to be totally devoid of novelty or intellectual remark, for they are as ancient as this external view of man. What is remarkable is that the race with singular accord and persistence has refused to accept them—this strange refusal has not been of the fair-weather variety. It is in just those crises of experience when nature gives the clearest demonstration of its power to swallow man up that man has issued his rejection of those claims..... For the major ceremonies of religion are so many gestures of defiance to the claims of nature. What is the most complete and universal assertion of nature's power over man? Death. What is the most universal and emphatic of all rites? The burial rite which is the ceremonial denial of that assertion." [6]

And it is among all primitive tribes, in every part of the world, that these burial rites are so striking and significant. The Kpelle tribe of Liberia build a hut over the grave of their chiefs and furnish it with all

[6] W. Cosby Bell, *If a Man Die*, p. 46.

the usual implements and weapons. The Shilluks have a similar custom.[7] The custom of dressing the dead in their best array and with ornaments or flowers is very widespread both in Africa and in Polynesia. In Togoland and on the island of Tahiti they dress their dead in fine clothing and cover them with garlands.[8] On the island of Nias they say, "The dead carry with them to the other world the shadows of all they possessed here." In many parts of the world the dead are regularly furnished with food and drink which is laid out or poured out, a libation on the grave. For fear that the spirits of the dead may return and work evil on the living, the corpse is tied fast, or maimed, or weighed down with heavy stones, or even in some parts of the world decapitated before burial.[9] In the New Hebrides and on the Solomon Islands the dead are carried far out to sea to prevent their spirits returning to their old dwelling-place. It is worthy of note that among many savage tribes in different parts of the world there still exists, as in very-ancient Egypt and ancient Europe, the custom of burying the dead in a doubled-up position as that of a child in the womb. This was intended to typify belief in a future birth into another life beyond the grave.[10]

In a careful analytical study of burial rites in every

[7] J. Witte, *das Jenseits im Glauben der Völker*, p. 9. Leipsig, 1924.
[8] *Ibid.*, pp. 11, 12.
[9] *Ibid.*, pp. 13-15. Cf. Warneck, pp. 59, 60.
[10] W. St. Clair Tisdall, *Christianity and Other Faiths*, p. 131.

ORIGIN OF BELIEF IN IMMORTALITY 217

part of the world, Miss Effie Bendann of the University of Chicago reaches the following conclusion:[11]

"The primitive seems to be concerned with the problem of life after death, if we may judge *from the prominence which this attitude assumes in the death-complex*. In many instances the kind of death determines the disposal of the body, the nature of life after death, the kind of offerings to be made to the deceased, and various ceremonials of a ritualistic character. . . . .

"As far as this investigation goes, the only elements which are exclusively characteristic of the death-situation are mourning-customs . . . . and the idea of life after death."

The writer of this interesting volume calls attention "to the universality of the notion that *death is unnatural*." Once death did not exist. It came by human error or by disobedience to the Divine Command. In the Caroline Islands they say, "Long, long ago death was unknown or it was a short sleep. . . . . But an evil spirit contrived the sleep of death."

"The following story is told by the Balolo of the Upper Congo to explain the continuance, if not the origin, of death in the world. One day, while a man was working in the forest, a little man with two bundles, one large and one small, went up to him and said, 'Which of these bundles will you have? The large one contains knives, looking-glasses, cloth and so forth; and the small one contains immortal life.' 'I cannot choose by myself,' answered the man; 'I must go and ask the other people in the town.' While he was gone to ask the others, some women arrived and the choice was left to them. They tried the edges of

[11] *Death Customs*, pp. 270, 282. New York, 1930.

the knives, decked themselves in the cloth, admired themselves in the looking-glasses, and, without more ado, chose the big bundle. The little man, picking up the small bundle, vanished. So when the man came back from the town, the little man and his bundles were gone. The women exhibited and shared the things, but death continued on the earth. Hence the people often say, 'Oh, if those women had only chosen the small bundle, we should not be dying like this!' " [12]

"Among various tribes in New South Wales it is said that men were supposed to live forever. They were forbidden to approach a certain tree where the wild bees made a nest. Despite many warnings, some women who coveted the honey attacked the tree with tomahawks. Whereupon out flew a bat which was Death. From now on it could claim all whom it could touch with its wings." [13]

The missionary Murray who traveled all across the Pacific island area in East Melanesia and New Guinea says: "I have never found in all my wanderings among savage tribes any who had not some idea of a future life." And Rosalind Moss, in a special detailed study of all the tribes of the Malay Archipelago, comes to the conclusion: "Thus we have only one authenticated instance of the denial of any future life and doubtful reports from some degraded Jakun people. The rites of these tribes seem to be of the nomadic forest-dweller type, namely abandonment before death and subsequent interment." Even here there may be animistic beliefs not yet tabulated.[14] The writer states that this uni-

[12] Frazer, *The Belief in Immortality*, vol. i, p. 472.
[13] E. Bendann, *Death Customs*, pp. 24, 26.
[14] *The Life After Death in Oceania*, p. 26. Oxford, 1925.

ORIGIN OF BELIEF IN IMMORTALITY

versal belief in a future life can be inferred from burial customs as far back as the glacial period. "The anthropologist can at least bear witness to the age-long and world-wide prevalence of the belief; leaving it to the philosopher to estimate the precise value of the argument from consent as best he may."[15]

There is indeed no question among present-day anthropologists as to the extreme antiquity of the belief in a future life after death. Some burials not only of the Upper but also of the Lower Palaeolithic Age appear to indicate that men at that period buried their dead with a dim and groping faith that for *them* life went on in some fashion beyond the grave. There is a famous example in the youth of the Neanderthal type found in the caves of Le Moustier in France. The position of his arms and weapons with bones of the wild ox split open for their marrow "make it appear reasonable," says John Murphy, "that these accompaniments of burial were intended as food and weapons for use after the change we call death."[16]

In the Fiji Islands there is a simple and pathetic custom of calling to the dead. The savage climbs a high tree or cliff and looking across the landscape mentions the name of a dead friend and exclaims: "Come back! come back!" There is a long period of time and of civilization between this cry and that of Tennyson in his poem *In Memoriam*, but the human heart is the

[15] *Op. cit.*, Foreword, p. ix.

[16] John Murphy, *Primitive Man: His Essential Quest*, p. 152. Oxford, 1927.

same everywhere. "Thou hast put eternity in their heart." [17]

Dr. John Murphy concludes his chapter on primitive belief in a future life with these eloquent words:

"In the background of this study we place frankly our theistic and Christian philosophy, which maintains that at the formless beginnings of the universe there is not merely the moving nebula but also God, and that God's way of clothing the lilies is by growth and wonderful transformation from the all but shapeless root down in the black earth. From this standpoint at least we perceive that even our apparent negative is but the reverse side of a positive, namely, that behind the inability to achieve the first distinct concepts, there is the ineradicable impulse to form concepts. And, indeed, there is behind it all, the unconquerable effort on man's part, as sharing in the tide-flow of the universe toward integration and differentiation, to attain unity in himself and in his world. In other terms, there is here the endeavour of man to make his life complete, to reach full 'self-realization,' which is the spark of the divine in the human and accounts for all man's progress. From this point of view, also, it is that the striking impression is gained of the immense spectacle of man in all ages from primeval times, with most rare exceptions, clinging to a belief in a world beyond this, and often following their dead into the mists which hide that world, not without love and hope." [18]

No one can read the long, long story of death and sorrow in the annals of the race—written on funeral urns and on tombs or in strange burial-rites, in the

[17] Eccles, 3:11, Hebrew text.
[18] *Primitive Man*, p. 163.

ORIGIN OF BELIEF IN IMMORTALITY 221

worship of ancestors, in the fear of returning spirits, in mutilations for the dead, in mourning as those who have no hope—no one can read this tragic story without realizing that there is a heart-hunger for eternity; and that there is a God and Father of all who knows and cares—who can have pity on the ignorant and those who are out of the way groping in darkness toward the Light . . . . because they are made in God's image and likeness.

> "Never a sigh of passion or of pity,
>   Never a wail for weakness or for wrong
> Has not its archive in the angels' city,
>   Finds not its echo in the endless song."

It is this universal belief in immortality, in a life beyond the present life that forms the best point of contact with non-Christians in the presentation of the Christian message. We preach Christ and the resurrection to those without Christ but not without a belief in a resurrection.

"A longing and seeking for God," says Warneck, "runs through the animistic heathen world like a vein of gold in the dirty rock." . . . . "The heart of the heathen is like a palimpsest, the original writing of which is written over and become unintelligible." [19]

We have seen that this *palimpsest of a primitive revelation to all mankind* included a knowledge of God, the idea of prayer and propitiatory sacrifice, the sanctity of monogamous marriage, and the sense of moral responsi-

[19] *The Living Christ and Dying Heathenism*, pp. 96, 98.

bility. We now can add that with the belief in immortality there was also the belief in another life in a world-to-come with rewards for the good and punishment for the evil. This is closely related to the various interpretations primitive peoples give of what takes place after death.

Some, such as the Shilluks, the Xosa-Kafirs, do not distinguish an immortality of the soul, but believe that body and soul together continue to live after death in accordance with their life here. A much larger number of primitives distinguish between soul and body and even teach that man has two souls, both of which live after death. The Tami of New Guinea say man has a "long soul" and a "short soul": the former wanders after death on earth; the latter enters the underworld. But the great majority of primitive peoples believe in one soul only which exists after the body decays and lives on. For a short time these undying spirits hover in the vicinity of the corpse and are to be feared, or propitiated or honored. Afterward they enter the realm of the hereafter.

Where is this located? Sometimes on distant islands or in high mountains, but generally under the earth. In Nias they call it "the city of the dead underground."[20] Among the Eskimos the rainbow is the bridge that leads to the sky and the better world. Others say it is the Milky Way that leads to it. Among many tribes the realm of the dead is in the far West where the sun sets. The Dyaks of Borneo place the

[20] J. Witte, *Das Jenseits im Glauben der Völker*, pp. 20, 21.

next world beyond a fabulous stream across which (as among the Greeks and Babylonians) a ferryman takes the soul. Therefore the coffin is often made in the shape of a canoe, as also among the Algonquin Indians.[21] Others speak of a narrow bridge from this world to the next. The Akpoto of Benue in Africa say it is as narrow as a sword's edge and a thousand years journey across! This latter may, however, be due to infiltration of Islamic eschatology.

The Eskimos picture heaven as a realm of light where there is no snow nor storm, no sorrow nor weariness, but only dancing and song.[22] The natives of Tahiti portray the future life of good souls as eternal joy in a realm of flowers and sunshine. The Indian of North America, as Pope reminded us,

> "Sees God in clouds and hears him in the wind.
> His soul proud Science never taught to stray
> Far as the solar walk, or milky way;
> Yet simple nature to his hope has given
> Behind the cloud-topt hill an humble heaven . . . .
> He thinks admitted to that equal sky
> His faithful dog shall bear him company."[23]

There is a beautiful touch in the eschatology of the Andaman Islanders. Not only have they a heaven for the warriors but a children's heaven. Here those who die young spend their days in heavenly meadows catching the birds of Paradise and feeding on ripe figs.[24]

---

[21] J. Witte, *op. cit.*, pp. 21, 22.
[22] *Ibid.*, p. 24.
[23] Pope, *Essay on Man*, part iii.
[24] J. Witte, *op. cit.*, p. 26.

But over against this almost universal belief in an abode of bliss for the good, the primitive also portrays in his legends and folk-lore a place of torment for the wicked. The Eskimos say "There is no sun there, but perpetual darkness, and howling storms of snow and ice." The tribes of Tartary picture hell as a place where the damned are choked by food they cannot swallow. The Ewe tribe believe that the fate of the avaricious miser is to have an abundance of cowrie-shells as money in the next world, but there is no food market! Unfaithful wives must eternally embrace thorn-bushes.[25]

Although not in all cases, yet among many primitives the rewards and punishments are based on moral grounds. The ethical standards of savages may be very different from our own, as among the head-hunters of Borneo, but even they still look forward to an after-life in accordance with *their ideas of moral desert*.

How powerful this belief in immortality is can be judged from the astonishing fact that in Samoa, the Fiji Islands, in parts of Africa, and among the Eskimos, the custom formerly prevailed of killing their aged relatives so as to hasten their entrance into a happy hereafter. And this to us cruel practice was welcomed by its victims as eagerly as modern science speaks of euthanasia.[26]

"When we try to sum up the ideas of the future life

---

[25] J. Witte, *op. cit.*, pp. 26, 27.

[26] *Ibid.*, p. 30. Cf. on this also Spiess, *Vorstellungen vom Zustände nach dem Tode*, pp. 54-110. Jena, 1877.

ORIGIN OF BELIEF IN IMMORTALITY

among primitives," says Spiess, "we conclude that although they are often sensuous and lowly, they are very seldom unworthy or impure. It is an established fact that there is no tribe or people that does not possess the expectation of a future life and none that places the end and goal of human life here on earth. In this fact we cannot help but recognize the gleam of an eternal truth." And he concludes that we cannot explain this primitive faith on any other ground than that of a Divine Voice in the soul or an instinctive urge of the emotions in the heart of man.[27]

The belief in immortality and in a final separation of man from man on an ethical basis seems almost too high an attainment for savage tribes descended from the cave-man according to science so-called. Yet facts are stranger than fiction.

"The father and mother of all fears," says Marett, "is, biologically speaking, the fear of death." But primitive man, instead of succumbing to this innate fear, met it squarely for thousands of years by an everlasting hope. He would not, he could not believe that death ends all. Rather death began all.

Marett draws a true picture of why heaven, hell, and a judgment were conceived by primitives:

"Now to consider in the first place the idea of hell, it is perhaps easier to find reasons why such a notion should have arisen than to account for the opposite belief in a happy hereafter, a heaven. For death encountered in the flesh is not a beautiful but a ghastly sight; nor, on the plane

[27] Spiess, pp. 172, 173.

of a merely animal intelligence, is its foulness anything but a warning to the living to keep away, seeing that human beings have not the entrails of hyenas. . . . .

"From this to an embryonic theory of retribution is but a step; for since one's friends are naturally good and one's enemies bad, unequal distribution of their future happiness seems to be eminently just. Finally, some sort of last judgment at which each soul must reap reward or punishment according to its personal and particular deserts is clearly conceived—so clearly, in fact, that an obliging savage will sometimes draw a map to show exactly where along the trail of the dead the stern judge stands and the path divides. It is to be noted, too, that such beliefs often occur among peoples of lowly culture amongst whom there is small opportunity for individuality to develop in a general way. Doubtless the explanation is that, as men die one by one, so they are held to be examined one by one." [28]

How close this natural religion comes to the words of the Apostle, "For we must all be made manifest before the judgment seat of Christ that each one may receive the things done in the body according to what he hath done, whether it be good or bad" (II Cor. 5: 10).

We come therefore once more to the question of the origin of this universal belief in immortality and judgment—to what the great anthropologist, Quatrefages, calls a "conviction that the existence of man is not limited to the present life but there remains for him a future beyond the grave." [29] If for no other reason than this, man surely deserves the name, *homo sapiens*.

[28] *Faith, Hope, and Charity in Primitive Religion*, pp. 65, 67.
[29] *The Human Species*, third edition, p. 484.

ORIGIN OF BELIEF IN IMMORTALITY

He knows God, although afar off, and he knows that his destiny is not that of the beasts which perish. He has an inkling of and a desire for a long home. When the golden bowl is broken and the silver cord is loosed and the mourners go about the streets after his dead, he is conscious of another life. Man has by nature a capacity for religion and a desire for immortality. These fundamental religious beliefs are, as Kellogg remarks, "held with an extraordinary universality, intensity, and persistency." They are unaccountable, except that there has been a subjective or objective revelation of God the Creator.[30]

God's voice in conscience, his image in man's intellectual and spiritual being, the faint reflection of his attributes in man's moral nature, so that we have a sort of faith, hope, and love even after the Fall, and among wild savages—all this is proof of a Revelation given to humanity in the beginning.

The Bible is the only book that gives an authoritative account, though in poetic language, of the origin of man and of his destiny, of his high calling, and of the revelation that came to fallen man. It is a book that has wide horizons, infinite stretches of space and time. It deals primarily, not with this life, but with a life yet to be. The great Pessimist of the Old Testament and the great Optimist Apostle of the New offer a sharp contrast in their personalities, environment, and mes-

[30] Kellogg, *The Genesis and Growth of Religion,* pp. 172-174. Cf. also the arguments of Walter Lippman in *A Preface to Morals,* pp. 41-45, that Modernists have "decoded" the biblical doctrine of immortality and left only an empty shell.

sage. But the writer of Ecclesiastes and Paul both insist that the present life is only vanity of vanities when compared with the life beyond. There is a time for everything and God hath made everything beautiful in its time. Yet all man's work and man himself must face a final judgment. The things that are seen are temporal, secular, only age-long; the things that are not seen are enduring, everlasting, and eternal.

The longing of the pagan soul is only satisfied by the Gospel of the Resurrection. St. Augustine's great word is true of the heathen heart everywhere: "Thou hast made us for thyself and our hearts find no rest until they rest in thee." That is why Jesus Christ in his teaching and Paul in his epistles continually lay emphasis on the eternal aspects of the present life, of the Church and of the missionary enterprise. Christ's parables have the background of the great day of judgment and deal with eternity. The parable of the Talents, of the Pounds, of the Ten Virgins, of the Wheat and the Tares, of Lazarus and Dives, of the Net, of the Great Supper—all are eschatological and refer to the life after death. Read Christ's last discourse in John's Gospel or his words on the end of the age in the Synoptics and you will realize that his horizon was distant and "beyond the river that has no bridge." Eternal life and eternal punishment cannot be eliminated from the teaching of Jesus. His Gospel of the resurrection at the grave of Lazarus rises far above the present earthly life. "What shall it profit a man," he said, on another occasion, "if he shall gain the whole world and lose his own soul?" To eat, to drink, to be merry, to forget the other world is the life of a fool. Here we sow, but "the harvest is the end of the world" for every one of us.

Paul's missionary message and passion were due to this vision of the eternal. "We look not at the things which are seen." "Knowing the terror of the Lord, we persuade men." "We must all appear before the judgment seat of Christ." "If in this life only we have hope in Christ we are of all men most miserable." Not only at Damascus, but all through Paul's life, "he could not see (earthly things) for the glory of that light"—which shone from the heavenly world.[81]

A social gospel without an otherworldly message will not attract or win even the most primitive races. They have the far-horizon. If even these aboriginal tribes long for a happy life across the River that has no bridge, we must emphasize the otherworldly character of our Gospel. The aim and goal of the missionary enterprise is not of the earth and earthly. John saw it on lonely Patmos—the great multitude which no man could number "of all nations and kindreds and peoples and tongues before the throne in white robes giving glory to the Lamb for ever and ever."

The three problems in anthropology to which evolution can offer no solution are those of the origin of sin and the dawn of conscience, the ineradicable desire for immortality, and the appearance on earth of a Sinless

---

[81] This and the preceding paragraph are taken from the writer's *Thinking Missions with Christ*, pp. 129-131.

One who wrought redemption by his death and resurrection.

In the first volume of an interesting series of studies on Bible Characters, the late Dr. Alexander Whyte of Edinburgh speaks of Adam and the question of his origin. He emphasizes, as we have tried to do in these chapters, the clear distinction between biological evolution in the realm of science and evolution as an attempt to explain origins in religion. We may well close our study with his weighty words:

"As we are carried away by the spell of the great writers on evolution, we feel all the time that, after all has been told, there is still something unrecognized and undescribed from which we suffer the most disturbing and injurious influences. All the time we feel in ourselves a backward, sideward, downward, perverse pull under which we reel and stagger continually; it is an experience that makes us wiser than all our teachers in some of the most obscure, but at the same time some of the most certain matters of mankind and their spiritual history. Speaking for myself, as I read the great books of our modern scientific men with a delight and an advantage I cannot put enough words upon, I always miss in them—in them all and in the best of them all—a matter of more importance to me than all else they tell me. For, all the time I am reading their fascinating discoveries and speculations, I still feel in myself a disturbance, a disorder, a disharmony, and a positive dislocation from the moral, and even from the material, order of the universe around me and above me: a disorder and a dislocation that my scientific teachers neither acknowledge nor leave room for its acknowledgment or redress. That is magnificent! That is noble!

ORIGIN OF BELIEF IN IMMORTALITY

That is divine! I exclaim as I read. But when I come to the end of my reading—Is that all? I ask. I am compelled by all my experience and all my observation to ask, Is that all? Is that your very last word to me? Then, if that is all, I must go still in search of a philosophy of nature and of man that understands me, and accounts for me, and has, if so be, a more comprehensive, a more scientific, a more profound, and a more consoling message to me. In one word, and to speak out of the whole of my disappointment and complaint in one word, What about *sin?* What is *sin?* When and where did *sin* enter in the evolution of the human race and seize in this deadly way on the human heart? Why do you all so avoid and shut your eyes to *sin?* And, still more, what about *Jesus Christ?* Why do I find nothing in your best textbooks about *him* who was *without sin?* About him who is more to me, and to so many more of your best readers, than all Nature, and all her suns, and systems, and laws, and processes put together? Far more. For he has carried both our understanding and our imagination and our heart so absolutely captive that we cannot read with our whole heart the best book you have written because his name is not in it. *Who* and *what* is *he,* we insist, who has leaped at a bound above all law and all order of matter and of mind, and of cosmic and ethic evolution, and has taken his stand of holiness at the head of the human race?"

L'ENVOI

THESE lectures had been delivered and the chapters completed when we had the honor and pleasure of a visit from Professor Wilhelm Schmidt. Accompanied by a distinguished German mathematician, he was on his way to China for further anthropological research, and on April 2 gave a remarkable lecture for us in Miller Chapel. It was an answer to a question whether the sixth volume of his work, *Der Ursprung der Gottesidee*, when it appeared, would give a synthesis of his argument and "tell us whence the relatively high religion of the oldest primitive peoples might have come." The substance of this important summary we give as follows. The whole argument is found in the final volume of Dr. Schmidt's work, which appeared later.

The answer to the question about the origin of the oldest religions, he said, is from three sources: first, from the testimony of primitive men themselves; second, from the content of their religions; and, third, from the causal and final ways of thinking in these religions.

If we turn, as seems quite natural, first to primitive men themselves, the reply they give leads always in the direction that they have not acquired religion by their own thinking and research, but by oral tradition from their fathers and forefathers, and finally from the Creator. Among the oldest of these tribes there are traditions that the Creator himself lived, after the creation, with men, and instructed them in their religious, social, and moral obligations. Nowhere do we receive evidence that these religions were developed to a higher degree of perfection by men through their own searching and finding, but, on the contrary, there is decline and deterioration.

The content of primitive religion always includes two beliefs: that the Supreme Being is effectively good, i.e., kind in sentiment and solicitude, and he is also morally good, i.e., holy, both positively and negatively. Now of these two beliefs it is especially the latter which seems to be astonishing. For even though the morality of the earlier primitive peoples compares favorably with that of the later primary peoples, yet they were men with numerous failings. Thus in their own experience they could not find a being who in every respect was morally good; therefore the belief in such a High Being could not be the result of their own research.

Causal thinking in primitive man is accompanied by final thinking; therefore, with the same universality with which they believe that God has created the world, they affirm that he has given to this world created by him, its final goal and aim, and that aim is to glorify him and serve man. If perhaps it seems to be quite natural that *some* of these primitive peoples arrived at this belief, it is more difficult to explain by purely natural causes that this belief is adhered to by *all* these peoples. It is still more difficult to explain how limitations were imposed upon man in utilizing the objects of creation, i.e., to employ them with reverence and temperance and to communicate them freely to others. Quite impermeable to purely natural explanation remains also the offering of first-fruit sacrifices before making use of the animal and vegetable food acquired from the created world.

These people believe also that not only to the world but to man himself the Creator has given a final goal; after having finished life here on earth, man is destined to be with him for all eternity. It seems to me that this belief in its concrete form cannot have been acquired by purely natural reason and research.

Thus causal and final thinking of man certainly points out *some* of the beliefs of the oldest religions. But they do not *fully* open the door to the totality and universality of beliefs which are found in those religions. Moreover, purely natural causal and final thinking produces new enigmas and creates new problems which are difficult of solution by natural thinking and research. Therefore, it is clear to me that it does not furnish us the key for opening the door that leads into the innermost sanctuary of the oldest religions and fully reveals to us the secret of their first origin.

How and where shall we find this key?

There must have been something quite impressively powerful which was met by primitive man not all too long after the beginning of their natural thinking and searching and which became to him an innermost "experience," penetrating and exciting his whole soul, and generating by its overwhelming power that unity which we see in the oldest religion.

This cannot have been a purely *subjective event* in the soul of man, because that could have originated neither the power and unity of this religion, nor the clearness and firmness of its beliefs and forms of cult. Nor can it have been a purely *exterior event*, as it could not have then exercised such a deep influence upon the free will of man and produced therein such a firmness and clearness of thinking and doing.

Nay, it must have been a great and powerful personality which met them in those days, a personality which was also able to *attract* their intellect by luminous truths, to bind their will by high and noble commandments, and to win their hearts by ravishing beauty and goodness. And this personality cannot have been merely a product of their own thinking and imagination; for such a *subjective* creature could not have had the real power of producing the effects that we have seen in that oldest religion. It must have been a personality which in his true objective reality forced himself upon them from without, and which just by the virtue of *His* reality overpowered them and persuaded them.

There can be no doubt, said Dr. Schmidt, as to who this personality was, and, besides, these oldest peoples themselves tell us: It is the really existing Supreme Being, the real Creator of heaven, of earth, and of men themselves, who presented himself to men, his highest creatures, and revealed himself to their thinking and willing and feeling, revealed to them his being and acting, directly after the creation when he lived with men on earth in familiar communication.

And it is to this conclusion that we are also led by the evidence of anthropology and the explicit witness of the Scriptures; the origin of religion is not by evolution but by revelation.

CLASSIFIED SELECT BIBLIOGRAPHY

THE entire attempt to formulate universal laws upon the basis of the intensive study of a very limited group of cultural facts literally bristles with fallacies and insupportable presuppositions, the most obvious and far-reaching of which embodies the idea that the ethnographic phenomena found in some specially selected area are the result of an independent development, and constitute, as it were, an indigenous entity possessing complete historic individuality."

"A suppressed element of irrefragable absurdity lies behind the attempt to frame evolutionary hypothesis on the basis of tribes alleged to be most primitive and, therefore, to constitute the elementary stage in the process of development. In any particular case, it is perfectly possible that the specific people involved has not wilfully contrived to remain in *statu quo*, in a chrysalis stage, for untold ages, and so provide the convenient basis for speculative reconstructions of the order of development, but on the other hand, may represent a process of degeneration from a higher level of culture."

SCHLEITER,
RELIGION AND CULTURE, *pp.* *10, 19.*

CLASSIFIED SELECT BIBLIOGRAPHY

THE following bibliography includes the most important works consulted on the subject. It has been classified into a General List which includes works on the History of Religion, followed by a list of books on each of the chapters for special reading. This classification necessarily overlaps, although each book is entered once only. The most important books are marked with an asterisk.

I. THE HISTORY OF RELIGION IN GENERAL

*B. ALKEMA and T. J. BEZEMER, *Volkenkunde van Nederlandsch-Indië*. Haarlem, 1927.
*COMTE GOBLET D'ALVIELLA, *Croyances, Rites, Institutions*. 3 vols. Paris, 1911.
*JOHN CLARK ARCHER, *Faiths Men Live By*. New York, 1934.
JOHN BACHELOR, *The Ainu of Japan*. New York, 1903.
*K. L. BELLON, *Inleiding tot de Vergelijkende Godsdienstwetenschap*. Mecklen, 1932.
*ALFRED BERTHOLET und EDWARD LEHMANN, *Lehrbuch der Religionsgeschichte*. 2 vol. Tübingen, 1925.
ALFRED BLUM-ERNST, *Wurms Handbuch der Religionsgeschichte*. Stuttgart, 1929.
A. R. RADCLIFFE-BROWN, *The Andaman Islanders*, Cambridge, 1933.
G. K. CHESTERTON, *The Everlasting Man*. New York, 1925.

242 CLASSIFIED SELECT BIBLIOGRAPHY

CARL CLEMEN, *Grundriss der Religionsphilosophie.* Bonn: Ludwig Röhrscheid, 1934.

CARL CLEMEN, *Religions of the World: Their Nature and Their History.* Tr. A. K. Dallas. New York, 1931.

*CARL CLEMEN, *Urgeschichtliche Religion* (Untersuchungen zur allgemeinen Religionsgeschichte, Heft 4). Bonn, 1932.

CARL CLEMEN, *Urgeschichtliche Religion.* Die Religion der Stein-, Bronze- und Eisenzeit. II. Abbildungen. Bonn; Ludwig Röhrscheid, 1933.

FRANK F. ELLINWOOD, *Oriental Religions and Christianity.* Ch. vii, "Traces of Primitive Monotheism." New York, 1892.

HORACE L. FRIESS and HERBERT W. SCHNEIDER, *Religion in Various Cultures.* New York, 1932.

*A. W. HOWITT, *The Native Tribes of South-East Australia.* London, 1904.

*LAWRENCE HYDE, *The Learned Knife.* An Essay on Science and Human Values. London: Gerald Howe Limited, 1928.

WILHELM IMMENROTH, *Kultur und Umwelt der Klein-Wuchsigen in Afrika.* Leipzig, 1933. (An account of the culture and social structure of Pygmy society.)

LOUIS HENRY JORDAN, *Comparative Religion: Its Genesis and Growth.* Edinburgh, 1905.

HENRI A. JUNOD, *The Life of a South African Tribe.* 2 vol. London, 1927.

*ALBERT C. KRUIJT, *Het Animisme in den Indischen Archipel.* The Hague, 1906.

BRUHL-LÉVY, *La Mentalité Primitive.*

CARL LUMHOLTZ, *Through Central Borneo.* 2 vol. New York, 1920.

*HENDRIK GERHARDUS LUTTIG, *The Religious System and Social Organization of the Herero.* Utrecht, 1934. (Testimony to the High-god among the Bantus.)

CLASSIFIED SELECT BIBLIOGRAPHY 243

*PAUL ELMER MORE, *The Sceptical Approach to Religion.* Princeton, 1934.

JOHN STRONG NEWBERRY, *The Rainbow Bridge:* A Study of Paganism. Boston, 1934.

GEORGE MCCREADY PRICE, M.A., *Modern Discoveries Which Help Us to Believe.* New York, 1934.

A. SPRENGER, *Alte Geographie Arabiens.* Bern, 1875.

W. ST. CLAIR TISDALL, *Christianity and Other Faiths.* London, 1912.

W. ST. CLAIR TISDALL, *Comparative Religion* (chapter on "Sacrifice"). London, 1909.

RICHARD CHENEVIX TRENCH, D.D., *Sermons Preached in Westminster Abbey.* New York, 1860.

GRACE H. TURNBULL, *Tongues of Fire:* A Bible of Sacred Scriptures of the Pagan World. New York, 1929.

*EDWARD B. TYLOR, *Primitive Culture.* 2 vol. London, 1920.

*JOH. WARNECK, *The Living Christ and Dying Heathenism.* Tr. Neil Buchanan. New York, n.d.

CLEMENT C. J. WEBB, F.B.A., *Religion and Theism.* London, 1934.

*GEORG WOBBERMIN, *The Nature of Religion.* Tr. Theophil Menzel and Daniel Sommer Robinson. New York, 1933.

WILLIAM KELLEY WRIGHT, *A Student's Philosophy of Religion.* New York, 1935.

SAMUEL M. ZWEMER, *Arabia the Cradle of Islam.* New York, 1892.

II. THE ORIGIN OF RELIGION

GRANT ALLEN, *The Evolution of the Idea of God.* New York, 1897.

*E. DENNERT, *Des geistige Erwachen des Urmenschen.* Erfurt, 1929. (An astonishing proof of the cultural attainment of man in the Stone-age.)

244 CLASSIFIED SELECT BIBLIOGRAPHY

*THEODORE GRAEBNER, *Essays on Evolution*. St. Louis, 1925.

A. M. HOCART, *The Progress of Man*. London, 1933.

E. WASHBURN HOPKINS, *Origin and Evolution of Religion*. New Haven, 1933.

*ROBERT H. LOWIE, PH.D., *Primitive Society*. New York, 1920.

NATHAN GRIER MOORE, LL.D., *Man and His Manor*. A History and an Outlook. Chicago: Privately Printed, 1935.

*LOUIS TRENCHARD MORE, *The Dogma of Evolution*. Princeton, 1925.

FRANCIS L. PATTON, *The Origin of Theism*. In the *Presbyterian Review*, pp. 732-760, New York, 1882.

CLIFFORD H. POPPER, *Chinese Religion through Its Proverbs*. Shanghai, 1926.

*W. SCHMIDT, *High Gods in North America*. Oxford, 1933.

*W. SCHMIDT, *The Origin and Growth of Religion:* Facts and Theories. Tr. H. J. Rose. New York, 1931.

W. SCHMIDT, *L'Origine de l' Idée de Dieu*. Articles in *Anthropos*, Vienna, 1908-1910.

*JOHN ROSS, *The Original Religion of China*. New York and Cincinnati, n.d.

*MICHAEL J. STOLEE, D.D., *The Genesis of Religion*. Minneapolis, 1930.

III. THE ORIGIN OF THE IDEA OF GOD

M. BLOOMFIELD, *The Religion of the Veda*. New York, 1908.

DE GROOT, *The Religion of the Chinese*.

*P. S. DESHMUKH, *Religion in Vedic Literature*. Oxford, 1933.

H. D. GRISWOLD, *The Religion of the Rigveda* (Farquhar

and Griswold, "The Religious Quest of India"). Oxford, 1923.
F. B. JEVONS, *The Idea of God in the Early Religions.*
*ALEXANDER LE ROY, *The Religion of the Primitives.* Tr. Newton Thompson. New York, 1922.
*R. H. LOWIE, *Primitive Religion.* New York, 1924.
JAMES HOPE MOULTON, *The Treasure of the Magi.* Oxford, 1917.
*JOHN MURPHY, *Primitive Man:* His Essential Quest. Oxford, 1927.
*W. SCHMIDT, *Der Ursprung der Gottesidee.* Münster, 1926-1934.
> Band I. Historisch-Kritischer Teil (with Bibliography).
> Band II. Die Religionen der Urvölker Amerikas.
> Band III. Die Religionen der Urvölker Asiens und Australiens.
> Band IV. Die Religion der Urvölker Afrikas.
> Band V. Nachträge zu den Religionen der Urvölker Amerikas, Asiens und Australiens, 1934.
>
> Band VI and VII (These give his conclusions.)

W. SCHMIDT, *Ein Versuch zur Rettung des Evolutionismus.* International Archiv für Ethnographie, Band xxix, Heft iv-vi. E. J. Brill, Leyden, 1928.
C. G. SELIGMANN, *The Veddas.* Cambridge, 1911. (The Veddas of Ceylon have been regarded as one of the most primitive of existing races.)

IV. THE ORIGIN OF THE WORLD AND OF MAN

HAROLD PEAKE, *The Flood:* New Light on an Old Story. New York, 1930.
*PAUL RADIN, *The Method and Theory of Ethnology.* London, 1933.
PAUL RADIN, *Primititve Man as Philosopher.* New York, 1927.

PAUL RADIN, *The Racial Myth*. New York, 1933.

*WILLIAM L. THOMAS, *Source Book for Social Origins. Ethnological Materials, Psychological Standpoint. Classified and Annotated Bibliographies for the Interpretation of Savage Society*. Chicago, 1909.

*BENJAMIN B. WARFIELD, "Antiquity and Unity of the Human Race" in *Studies in Theology*, pp. 235-258. New York, 1932.

WILLIAM WARREN, *Paradise Found. The Cradle of the Human Race at the North Pole. A study of the Prehistoric World*. Boston, 1885. (Fanciful theory.)

V. THE ORIGIN OF PRAYER AND SACRIFICE

F. C. BURKITT, *The Eucharistic Sacrifice*. Cambridge, 1921.

S. I. CURTISS, *Primitive Semitic Religion Today*. Chicago, 1902.

G. B. GRAY, *Sacrifice in the Old Testament*. Oxford, 1925.

L. W. GRENSTED, *A Short History of the Doctrine of the Atonement*. Manchester, 1920.

*HEILER, *Das Gebet*. München, 1923.

F. C. N. HICKS, *The Fullness of Sacrifice*. London, 1930.

*E. O. JAMES, *Origins of Sacrifice*. London, 1935.

*E. O. JAMES, *Primitive Ritual and Belief*. London, 1917.

Jewish Encyclopedia, art. "Sacrifice."

A. LANG, *Myth, Ritual and Religion*. London, 1887.

W. R. SMITH, *The Religion of the Semites* (3rd ed.). London, 1927.

*H. C. TRUMBULL, *The Blood Covenant*. London, 1887.

VI. THE ORIGIN OF FIRE-WORSHIP AND FIRE AS A SYMBOL OF DEITY

E. G. CUTHBERT and F. ATCHLEY, *A History of the Use of Incense*. London, 1909.

CLASSIFIED SELECT BIBLIOGRAPHY 247

SIR JAMES GEORGE FRAZER, *Myths of the Origin of Fire*. London, 1930.

*WALTER HOUGH, *Fire as an Agent in Human Culture*. Washington, 1926.

ADALBERT KUHN, *Die Herabkunft des Feuers und des Göttertranks*. Gütersloh, 1886.

J. MAES, *Les Allume-Feu du Congo Belge*. Bruxelles, 1933.

Studi e Materiali di Storia delle Religioni, vol. v, art. on "La festa del Fuoco sacro in Babilonia," by Guiseppi Furlani. Rome, 1928.

T. CATO WORSFOLD, *The History of the Vestal Virgins of Rome*. London, 1932.

VII. THE ORIGIN OF MARRIAGE AND PRIMITIVE ETHICS

HELEN BOSANQUET, *The Family*. London, 1915. (On the meaning and importance of the family as an institution. The first part deals with the prehistoric family.)

J. H. BREASTED, *The Dawn of Conscience*. New York, 1934.

A. E. CRAWLEY, *The Mystic Rose*. A study of primitive marriage. London, 1905.

FREDERICK ENGEIS, *The Origin of the Family*. Chicago, 1910.

J. FRAZER, *Totemism and Exogamy*. London, 1910.

*BRUNISLAW MALINOWSKI, art. "Marriage" in Encyclopedia Britannica, 14th Edition.

E. MALINOWSKI, *The Family Among Australian Aborigines*. London, 1913.

*R. R. MARETT, *Faith, Hope, and Charity in Primitive Religion*. New York, 1932.

R. R. MARETT, *Sacraments of Simple Folk*. London, 1933.

*HAROLD C. MORTON, *The Supposed Evolutionary Origin*

of the Moral Imperative. In the Journal of Transactions of the Victoria Institute, vol. lxv.
T. V. SMITH, *Beyond Conscience*. New York, 1934.
C. N. STARCKE, *The Primitive Family in Its Origin and Development*. New York, 1889.
N. W. THOMAS, *Kinship Organization and Group-Marriage in Australia*. 1906.
*EDWARD WESTERMARCK, *The History of Human Marriage*. London, 1891.
EDWARD WESTERMARCK, *The Origin and Development of the Moral Ideas*.
*EDWARD WESTERMARCK, *Three Essays on Sex and Marriage*. London, 1934. (The third essay is a reply to Briffault's criticism of his work on *Human Marriage*, reasserting his theory of primitive monogamy.)
W. C. WILLOUGHBY, *Nature Worship and Taboo*. Hartford, 1932.

VIII. THE ORIGIN OF BELIEF IN IMMORTALITY

EFFIE BENDANN, *Death Customs:* An Analytical Study of Burial Rites. New York, 1930.
*CARL CLEMEN, *Das Leben nach dem Tode im Glauben der Menschheit*. Leipzig und Berlin, 1920.
*J. G. FRAZER, *The Belief in Immortality and the Worship of the Dead*. London, 1913.
*J. G. FRAZER, *The Fear of the Dead in Primitive Religion*. London, 1933.
R. R. MARETT, *The Threshold of Religion*. 1909.
ROSALINE MOSS, *The Life after Death in Oceania and the Malay Archipelago*. Oxford, 1925.
*EDMUND SPIESS, *Entwicklungsgeschichte der Vorstellungen vom Zustande nach dem Tode*. Jena, 1887.
WILLIAM TEMPLE (Archbishop of York), *The Idea of Immortality in Relation to Religion and Ethics*. London, 1932.

INDEX

A

Abel's Offering, 154
Abraham's smoking furnace, 154
Acts 14: 15-17, 198
Adam, 69, 96, 156
Adi, Sheikh, founder of Yezdi sect, 169
Aeschylus, *Prometheus Bound,* 170
Agni, 153, 159
Ahura Mazda, 87, 166
Ainu of North Japan, 162 f.
Akbar, 31
Akpoto of Benue, Africa, 223
Algonquin Indians, 139, 145, 223
Allah, 90
Allier, Raoul, 65
Altar-fires, symbol of sacrificial worship, 172
Amen-Ra and Rat with golden disk, 176
American Indians, 61, 78, 115, 223
Ancient heathen religions, 47
Andaman Islanders, 108, 223
—creation-myth of, 117, 119
—have no prayer, 134
—monogamous, 187, 192
Anthropological misconceptions, 93
Antiquity of belief in future life after death, 219
Antiquity of man, 24
Arabs of ancient Arabia, 90
Arapaho Indians, 140
Archaeology and age of man, 12
Argument of the book, 12-14

Aristotle, 103
Ashur, worship of, 90
Assyria, 89
Atchley, E. G. Cuthbert, on incense, 174
Atkins, G. G., 54
Augustine, 128
—*City of God,* 31
Aztecs, 104

B

Bachelor, John, on fire-gods of Japan, 163
Bacon, Lord, 21
Bacon, Roger, 31
Baker, Karl Wilson, poem on flame of life, 174
Bantu race, nobility of, 200
Barth, Karl, 34
Barton, George A., says Semites not totemistic, 147
Battak proverbs, 83
Belief in immortality among primitives, 212
Bellon, K. L., 58
Beltane fires of Scotland and Ireland, 172
Bentham, 196
Berosos, 30
Bhakti, Hindu doctrine of, 45
Bible—and history of religion, 38
—on dawn of conscience, 194
Biblical scholarship and history of religion, 39
Black man's mind, 116
Blood sacrifice, 143

249

Boegner, Marc, 64
Bonfires in Celtic countries, 172
Bosman, 32
Brockelmann, D. C., on Arabian monotheism, 91
Brosses, 32
Browne, Lewis, 53
—on primitive society, 182
Buddhism, 44, 69
Bunsen, 27
Burial rites, 215
Bushmen, 145

C

Calvin's doctrine of the knowledge of God, 98
Cave-man, 182
Caves of Le Moustier, France, 219
—paintings, 144
Champollion, 33
Chaos to Cosmos, 103
Chastity, 188
Chesterton on sanctity of the family, 182
Cheyenne Indians, 140
Chinese Cosmogony, 105
Chinese faith, primitive, 144
Chinese Monotheism, 84
Christ, Jesus, 49
—came to baptize with fire, 155
—and the Resurrection, 221
—parables deal with eternity, 228
Christian religion, its character, 44
Christian Revelation, universality and finality of, 49, 232
Cicero, 103
Clarke, James Freeman, 103
Coleridge, *Aids to Reflection*, 122
Columbia Theological Seminary, 17
Comparative Religion, 29
Consanguineous unions taboo, 190

Conscience, 71
—nature of, 204
—related to God the Creator, 203
Conversion of Primitives, The, 65
Cosmogonies, 104
Crawley, A. E., 153
Creation, 22
Creation *ex nihilo*, 109
Creation of man, 117
—North Central California legend, 110
Creation-epic of Babylonia, 114, 174
Creation-myths, 13, 104
—and early chapters of Genesis, 114
—of Indian tribes, 106
Creation-story of Guatemala, 107
Creuzer, 32
Cultural levels, list of, 77
Culture, primitive, 35

D

Damaras of South Africa, 164
Dark, Sidney, on prayer gestures, 133
Darmesteter, 34
Darwinian theory, 57
David's altar, 155
Dawn of Conscience, The, 193
Death in primitive religion, 118
Death, origin of, 118, 217
—unnatural in primitive thought, 217
Degeneration, 240
—or deterioration of religion, 63
Delaware Indians, 139, 165
—prayer, 137
Demiurge as Creator, 112
Dostoievski, *The Brothers Karamozov*, 209
Driesch, Professor, 22
Duperron, 33

INDEX

Durkheim, 34
Dyaks of Borneo, 222

E

Ecclesiastes and Paul on present and future life, 228
Egyptian Monotheism, 89
Elijah on Mount Carmel, 155
Eskimos, 145, 222
Ethical code of Bavili tribe, 201
Ethics, primitive, 116
Etruscan inscriptions show belief in immortality, 211
Evolution, 22, 52, 55, 63, 105, 120, 197
—the latest word on, 121
Evolution, Emergent, 196, 197
Evolution or Revelation, 196
Evolutionary concept, 59
Evolutionary hedonism, 196
Evolutionary hypothesis, 35, 240
—rejected, 56
Evolutionary theory, 57
Ewe tribe, 224
Exogamy, origin of, 195
—almost universal, 189
Expiation, 127
Ezekiel's vision, 155

F

Fahrenfort, J. J., reply to Schmidt, 37
Fairbairn, Principal, 27
Faith, Hope, and Charity in Primitive Religion, 194
Family as a social unit, 183
—the central pillar of social life among primitives, 189
Father, name applied to Supreme Being, 62, 79
—in primitive prayer, 136
Fatherhood of God among primitives, 131
Fear of the Dead in Primitive Religion, The, 69
Fetishism, first book on, 32
Fiji Islanders, calling the dead, 219

Fire—origin in human culture, 13, 157
—in Scripture, 156
—in Jewish tradition, 156
—as agent in human culture, 158
—as purifier, 164
—in Brahman religion, 167
—as method of communion with God, 171
Fire-baptism, 175
Fire-drill and fire-saw, 158
Fire-gods, 162
—of Pueblo Indians, 162
—in China, 168
—also light-gods, 175
Fire-making, primitive methods, 158
Fire-origin myth — of Eskimo, 160
—of Maori, 160
—of Sioux Indians, 161
Fire-temples, 166
Fire-worship — and fire as a symbol of deity, 153 ff.
—and fetishism, 157
—and fire-ritual widely diffused, 162
Flints in Palaeolithic age, 158
Flood - story in Zoroastrian Scriptures, 111
Flood-tradition — Harold Peake on, 113
—universality of, 112
Frankincense trade of antiquity, 173
Freudian behaviorism, 204
Funeral customs, earliest stage, 68
Future life in New Guinea, 218
Future state of existence after death, 209 ff.

G

Gabun Pygmies, 116
Gairdner, Temple, 47
Gallas of East Africa, 138

Gardner, Percy, on eating of sacrifice, 143
Genesis, 56, 71, 104, 111, 113, 119
—Adam's coat of skin, 147
—on origin of marriage, 183
Gideon's sacrifice, 154
God of Sinai, 56
God made of fire among primitives, 163
God, the Eternal Torment of Man, 64
God's ministers flames of fire, 156
God's voice in conscience, 227
Golden Age, 93, 118 f.
Gospel of the resurrection, 228
Graf-Wellhausen Bible critics on immortality in Old Testament, 212
Great Spirit called Father-of-All, 129
Greek cosmogonies, 114

H

Halo, the, 175 ff.
Head-hunters of Borneo monogamous, 192
Heart of heathen like palimpsest, 221
Hearth-fire, 165, 171
Heaven of primitive religion, 223
Heaven, hell, and judgment conceived by primitives, 225
Hebrew religion, 55
Hegel, 27, 32
Heiler on prayer, 135 ff.
Hell in primitive religion, 224
Herbert, George, poem on Prayer, 126
Herodotus, 30, 90
High-gods, 63, 78, 95
—primitive, 61
—attributes of 81, 109
—among all primitive tribes, evidence for, 84

—or Sky-god, 198
—has moral character, 202
High-gods in North America, 62
Hinduism, 44
Historical method, 12, 61
History of religion 26, 28
—divisions of, 28
—summary, 30
—value of, 40, 47
History of religions, 29
History of the history of religion, two theories, 13 ff.
Hocking, W. E., comments on Bertrand Russell's view, 215
Homo sapiens, 12, 68, 95, 121, 208, 226
Hooker, 103
Howitt, 35
Hume, David, 32 196

I

Ibn-al-Arabi on Deity of Christ, 46
Immortality of the soul 14, 69, 209 ff.
Incarnation, 49
Incense—in worship, 173 ff.
—in Babylonia, 174
—in Israel, 174
Incest, 146
—the sin of sins, 190
Inspiration and revelation, 45
Isaiah's vision, 155
Islam, 45 f., 69
—history of, 29
—in Sumatra, 45
Isoka Tribe in Nigeria, 81, 146
Ituri-Pygmies of Central Africa, 108
Izanagi-no-mikoto, 105

J

Jain, Champat Rai, quoted on immortality of soul, 211
Jainism and future life, 211
James E. O., on origin of sacrifice, 142

INDEX

Japanese feast of lanterns, 175
Jerrold Douglass, 12
Jerusalem Council, 40
Jevons, 34
Jewish Nur-Tamid, 175
Job, 102
Judaism, 44
Judgment seat of Christ, 226

K

Kaaba 90
Karubars, 193
Kato, Genchi, on monotheism in Japan, 86
Keith, A. Berriedale, quoted, 20
Kekchi Indians, 138
Kellog, Dr., 95
Kiel on Genesis 3: 21, 149
Killing of aged relatives to hasten their entrance into a happy hereafter, 224
Kruijt, 36
Kulin of Australia, 108

L

Lang, Andrew, 14, 76, 212
Langdon, 15
Lehmann, 30
Le Roy, *Religion of the Primitives*, 42
Leviticus 10: 1-3, Nadab and Abihu, 172
Libanotopheros Regio, 173
Lippman, Walter—on the Golden Age, 119
—*Preface to Morals*, 195
Livingstone, instances of kindness and unselfishness, 199
Lodge, Oliver, 22
Lowie, Robert H., 59, 183
Lubbock, 34
Lupercalia at Rome, 175
Luther on Genesis, 123

M

Magic—and prayer, 135
—in religion, 146
Maidu fire-myth, 160

Malinowski on monogamy, 185
Man—in the universe, 95
—origin of, 21, 103 ff.
—vs. monkey among Pygmies, 117
—primitive, 122
—primitive, causal thinking of, 234
Maori poem of creation, 108
Marett, R. R.—on promiscuity vs. monogamy, 180
—or racial unity, 25
Marriage among Australian aborigines, 191
Marxist ideology, 204
Materialism, breakdown of, 22
Mauss, 36
Mexican prayer, 131
Miao race of China, 80
Michelangelo, *Creation of Adam*, 116
Mill, 196
Missionary enterprise, 40
—not merely social, 229
Modi, Jivaniji Jamshedji, on customs of Parsees, 152
Mohammedanism, 44
Monogamy, 186
—earliest form of marriage, 68
—most common form of human marriage, 188
Monotheism, 37, 56, 64
—primitive, 13, 65, 77
—primitive, in Japan, 86
Moral idea and moral ideals, 198
—origin of, 193 ff.
More, Paul Elmer, 71
—on creation-myths and early chapters of Genesis, 114
Morton, Harold C., quoted, 197
Moses at burning bush, 154
Moslems, 31
Mother-love in primitive races 200
Müller, Max, 27, 33
Murphy, John, 220
Myths regarding origin of fire, 159

N

Nadab and Abihu (Lev. 10: 1-3), 172
Nassau, Robert H., on monotheism, 79
Neanderthal man, 68, 120
New Testament, universal outlook of, 48
Nimbus in pagan and Christian art, 175, 177
Nirvana, 210
Non-Christian religions, 41, 43
—reveal primitive revelation, 130
Non-Christian thought, 45

O

Oesterly, 40
Offering of tobacco smoke, 173
Old and New Testament on fire as symbol, 153
Old Testament, 47
—importance of, 42
—prophets of, 48
—doctrine of Immortality, 213
Omaha Indians, 79
Orang-utan, family life of the, 192
Ordeal by fire, 175
Orelli, 34
Original sin, 194
Ottawa Indians invoke Great Spirit, 140

P

Paleolithic period, 144
—religion of, 68
Parallels to Genesis, 116
Parsi religion, 166
—custom of fire-worship, 152
Passover, 55
Patton, Francis L., 96
Paul and Ecclesiastes on present and future life, 228
Paul and natives of Melita, 200
Paul's missionary message and passion, 229

Parliament of Religions, Chicago, 31
Pentecost, tongues of flame, 155
Pillar of fire, 154
Plato on prayer, 130
Pleistocene period, 121
Plopper, Clifford H., on fire-gods in China, 168
Plutarch, 30
—on prayer, 130
Polo, Marco, 32
Prayer—and sacrifice, 13
—primitive, 126
—primitive, examples, 137
—primitive, addressed to a Supreme Being, 129
—its antiquity and universality, 127 ff.
—and magic, 128, 132
—nature of, 130
—prior to magic, 133
—content of among primitives, 134
—examples of, 134
—posture in, 135
—to spirits of forest, 135
—before meals, 140 f.
—of Chinese Emperor, 141
—to Mexican fire-god, 162
Predestination, 45
Primitive Culture, 33
Primitive Monotheism in China, 85
Primitive Society, 59
Primitives, virtues of, 201
Prometheus, 159, 170
Promiscuity and the origin of marriage, 183
Puglisi, Mario, on prayer, 132
Pygmies, 61, 108, 145

Q

Quatrefages, 26

R

Ra, Sun-god of Egypt, 153
Rabbinical legend about fire, 156
Rabin, Israel, 55

Rainbow Bridge, The, a recent book on history of religion, 181
Rask, 33
Redan, 56
Reinach, 34
Religion—defined, 30
—of primitive tribes, five elements of, 70
—degeneration of, 74, 76
—origin of, 26
—primitive, 30, 234
Religion of the Primitives, 42
Religion of the Semites, 34
Renan, Ernest, 33
—on Genesis, 122
Resurrection, belief in at time of Christ, 214
Revelation, 96, 236
—primitive, 196, 227
—primitive, subjective or objective, 205
Réville, 34
Richards, Timothy, 84
Rig-Veda, 86, 102, 159
Romans, chapter 1, 16, 56, 71
—4: 14, 15; 198
Ross, John. *Primitive Monotheism in China*, 85
Routledge, account of African prayer, 139

S

Sabaeans, 169
Sacrifice—and prayer, 127 ff.
—origin of, 141 ff.
—in China, 144
—classification of, 145
—Biblical origin of, 148
St. Gabriel Scientific Institute, 36
Samoyeds of the Arctic, 108
Santals, 193
Saussaye, Chantepie de la, 34
Saxo, 31
Sayce, A. H., on creation-epic, 114
Schelling, 27, 32

Schleiter, Frederick, 58
Schmidt, Wilhelm, 14, 16, 57
—his life and works, 36
—book reviewed and analyzed, 60
—summary of argument, 233
Semang Pygmies, 108, 117, 146
Seminoles, 115
Seneca's prayer, 131
Sexual love among animals, 184
Sex-worship, 105
Shahrastani, 31
Shangti, the Supreme Ruler, 106
Shilluks, 222
Shinto cosmogony, 105
Sin—in primitive society, 201
—origin of, 231
—and death, origin of, 118
Sioux Indians, 165
Sky-god, 94
—among primitive tribes, 75
Smith, Robertson, 34
Smyth Foundation, 17
—theory of sacrifice, 146
Söderblom, Archbishop, 27
Soper, E. D., 54
Sophocles, *Antigone*, and ordeal by fire, 176
Spencer, Herbert, 33, 197
—Unknowable First Cause, 23
Stephen, 176
Stone Age, 59
—religion of, 26, 144
Strabo, 31
Sun-worship allied to fire-worship, 165
Supreme Being and First Father, 62
—author of moral code, 203

T

Taboos and totemism, 13
Tacitus, 31
Tahiti hymn of creation, 109
Tami of New Guinea, 222
Tanner, John, captured by Indians, 140

Tennyson—on immortality, 210
—*In Memoriam*, 219
Theism—origin of, 96
—natural and revealed, 97
—in early Egypt, 113
Thoth as Creator, 113
Tibetan prayer wheel, 132
Tiele, 34
Toland, John, 32
Torah a book of fire, 156
Totemism, 34, 63, 142, 181
—defined, 146
—a family pact, 147
—in close relation to exogamy, 189
—strengthens family bond, 190
Totemistic theory rejected, 15
Tower of Silence, 166
Transfiguration, The, 177
Tree of Life, The, 154
Trench, Archbishop, 23, 147
Tribes, primitive, 77
Trinity, The, 45, 47
Tutankhamen's tomb and belief in future life, 211
Tylor, 33
—on fire-worship, 157

U

Unity of God, 46
Unity of the race, 24 ff.
Universe, greatness of, 11
Ursprung der Gottesidee, Der, 57, 77
Utilitarian philosophy, 196

V

Van Gennep, 36
Vancouver Island, 165
Varro, 31

Varuna, prehistoric Sky-god, 86
—Creator of the universe, 114
Veddas, 145
—monogamous, 187, 191
Vesica piscis, aureole, 177
Vestal virgins, 169-171
Voltaire, 27, 32

W

Warfield, Dr., on unity of race, 24
Warneck, Johannes, *The Living Christ and Dying Heathenism*, 82
Westermarck—on substitution in blood sacrifices, 143
—on marriage, 184 ff.
Whyte, Alexander, on Adam and question of his origin, 230 f.
Winnebago Indians, 110
Wobbermin, George, on primitive monotheism, 83
Wood, Irving F., on the 'Bible as source-book, 38
World, origin of the, 104 ff.

X

Xosa-Kafirs, 222

Y

Yahweh, 89
Yezdis of Mesopotamia, 169

Z

Zeus-Pater, 115
Zionism, 44
Zoroaster, 110, 165
Zoroastrianism, 87, 154, 167
—paradise, 111
—fire-worship, 152

www.ingramcontent.com/pod-product-compliance
Lightning Source LLC
Chambersburg PA
CBHW071428150426
43191CB00008B/1078